This Book is dedicated to all family and friends that have always inspired and supported my art. To all of them past and present keep creating.

Thank you, JV

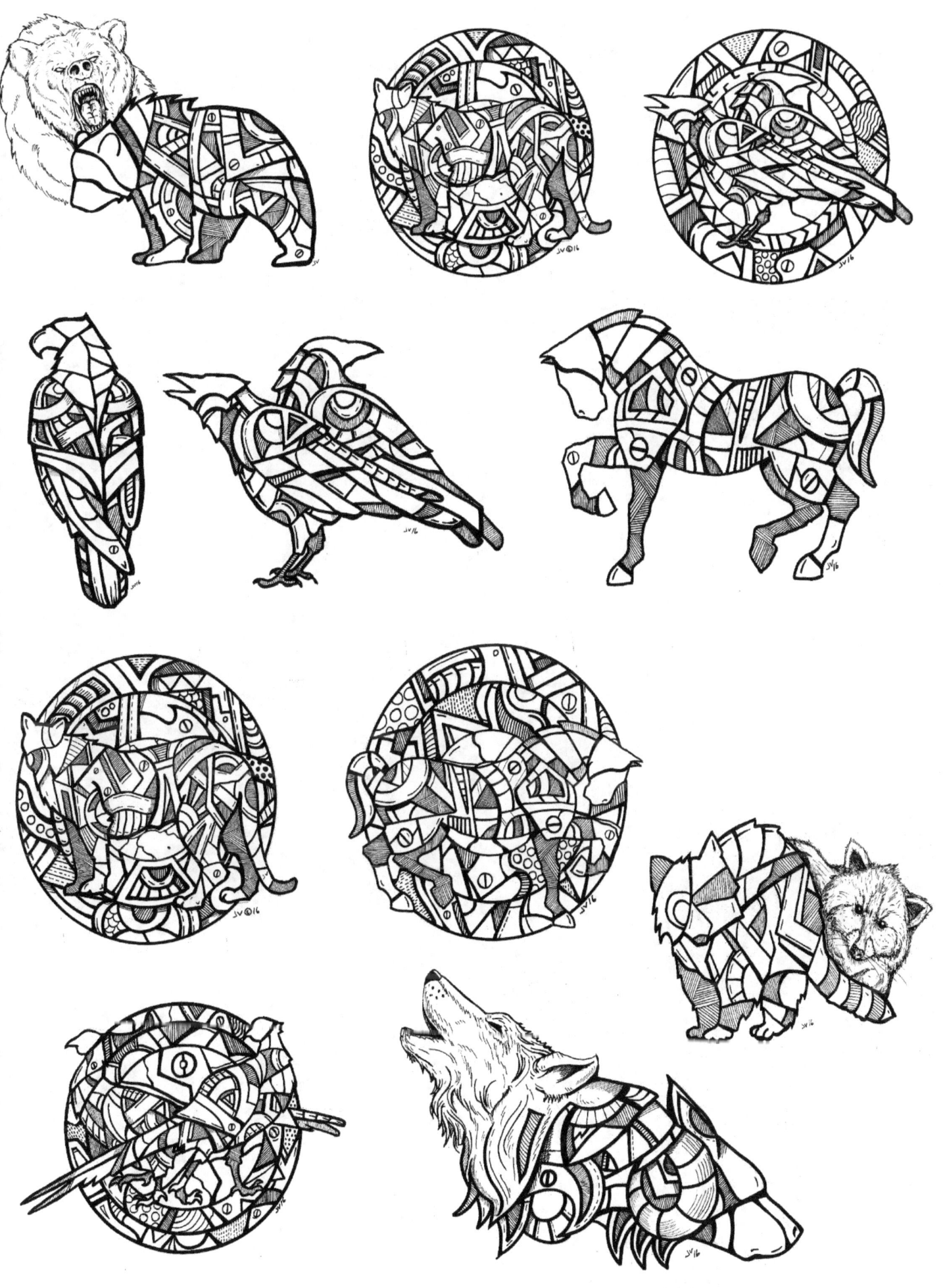

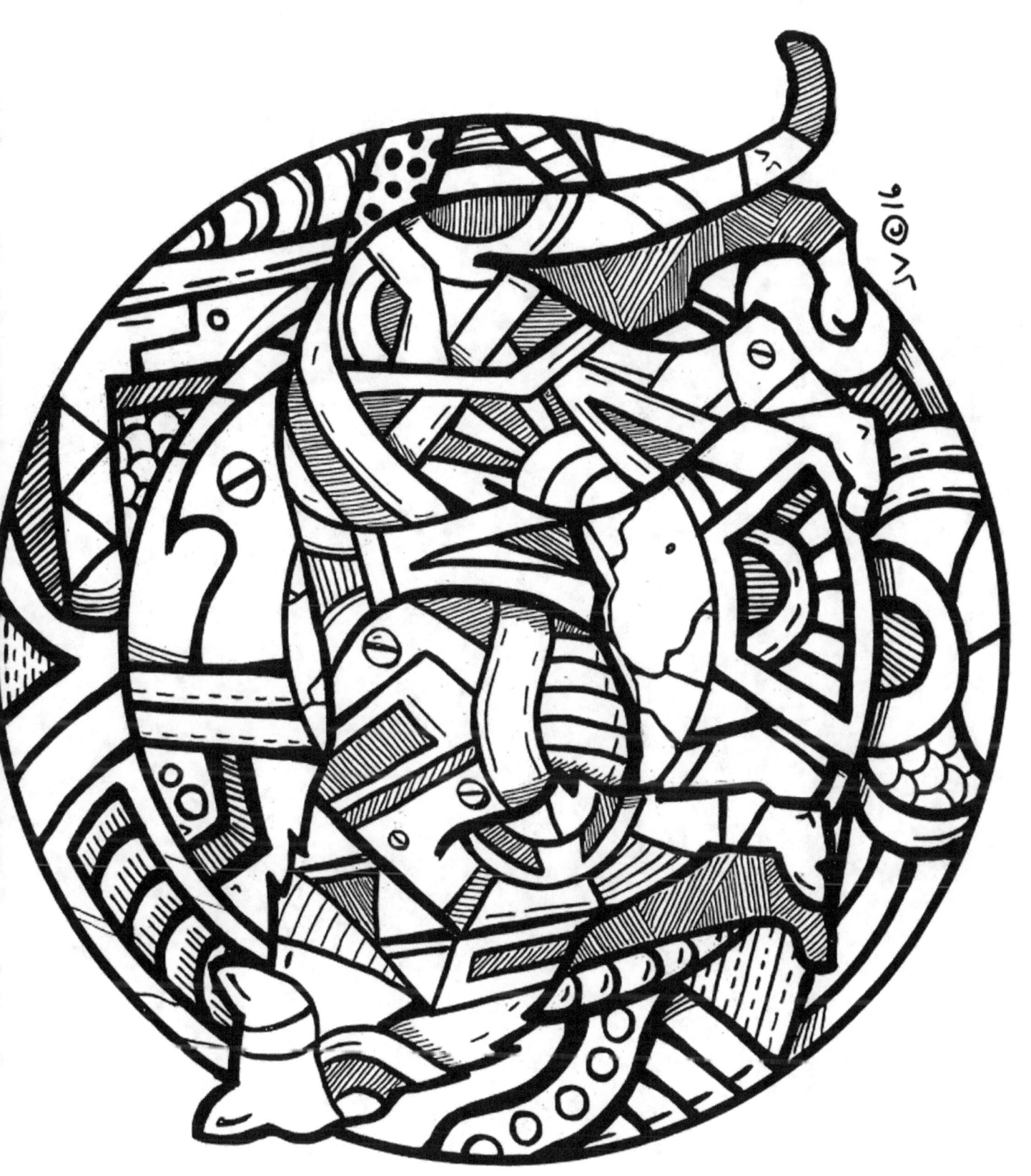

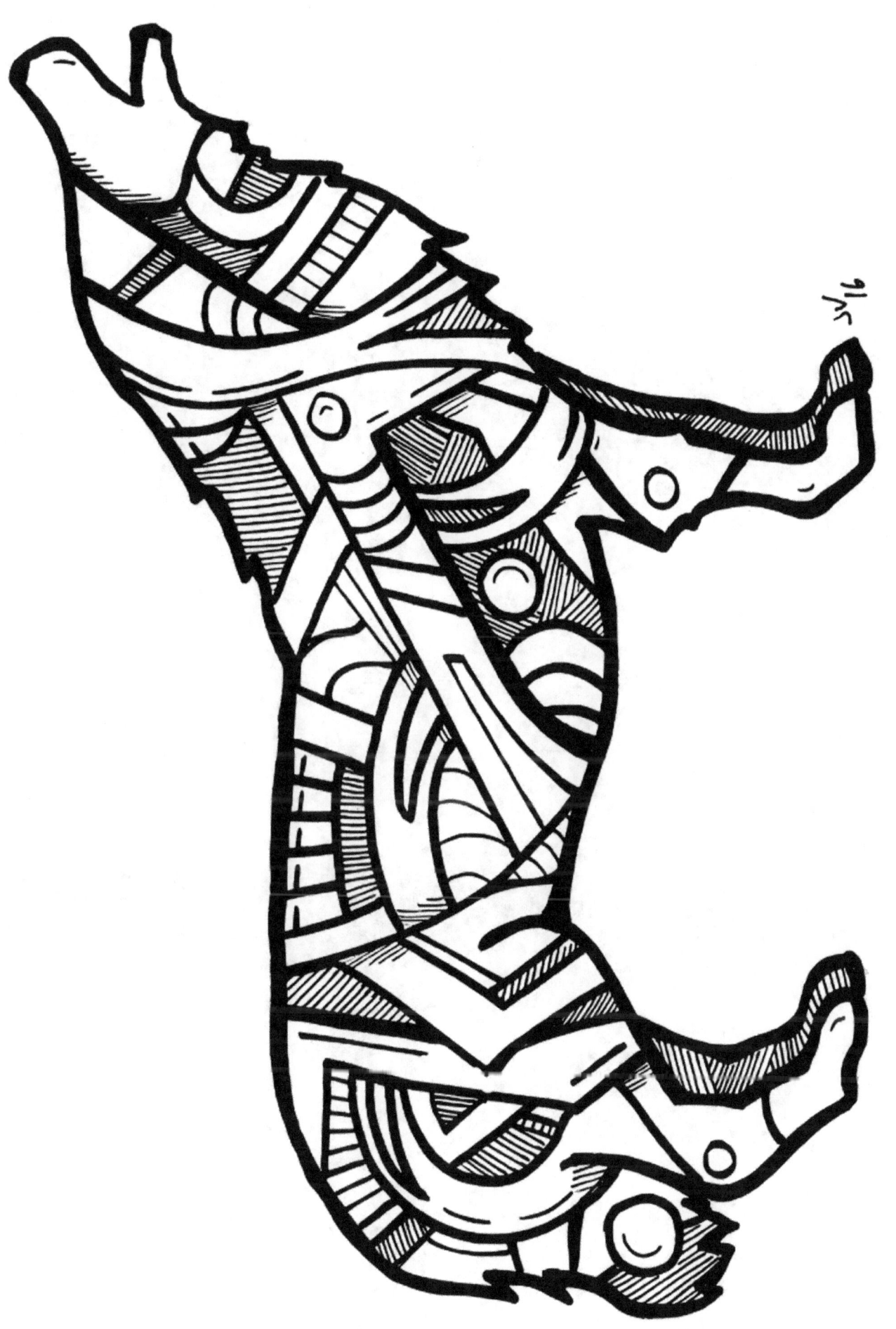

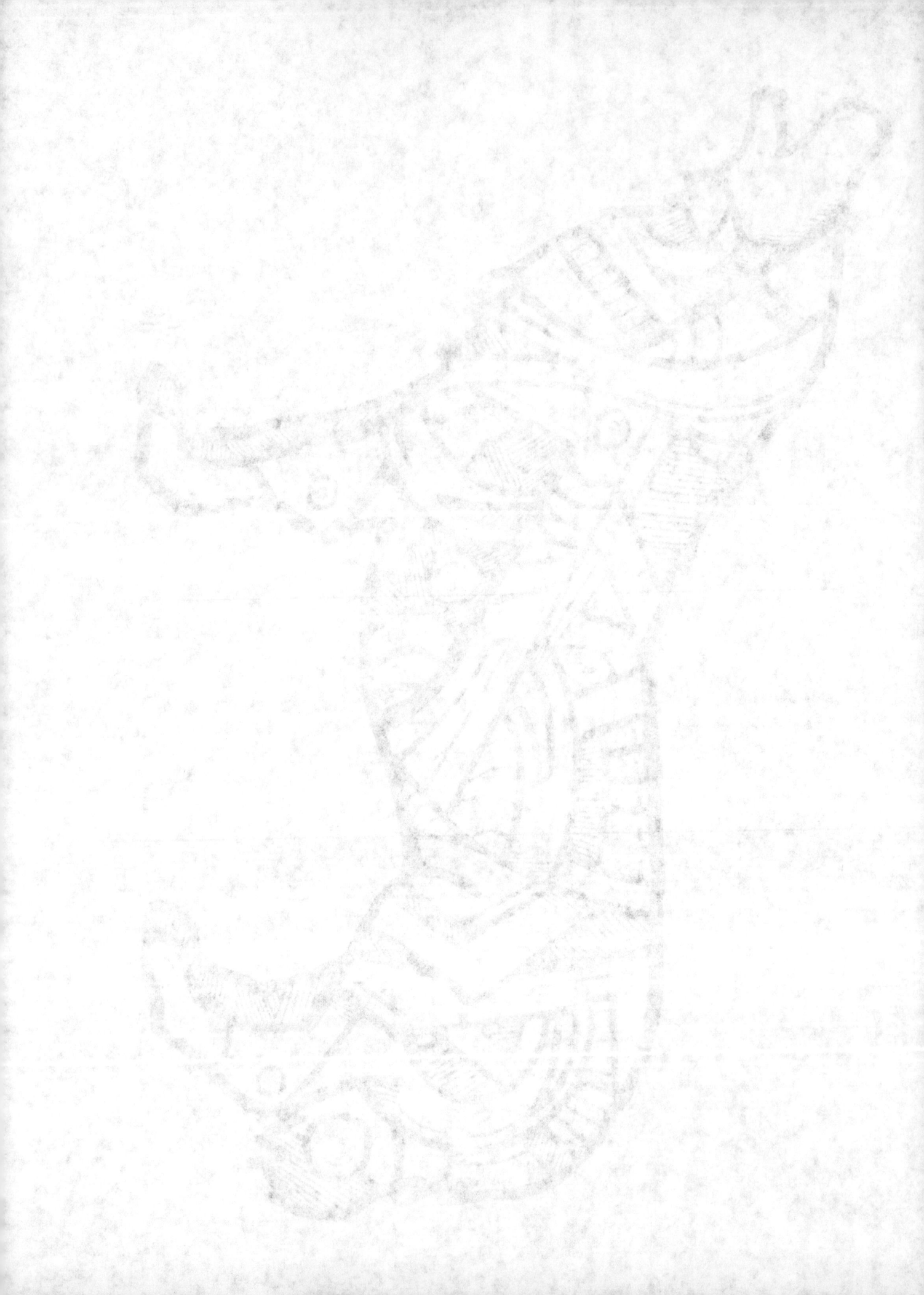

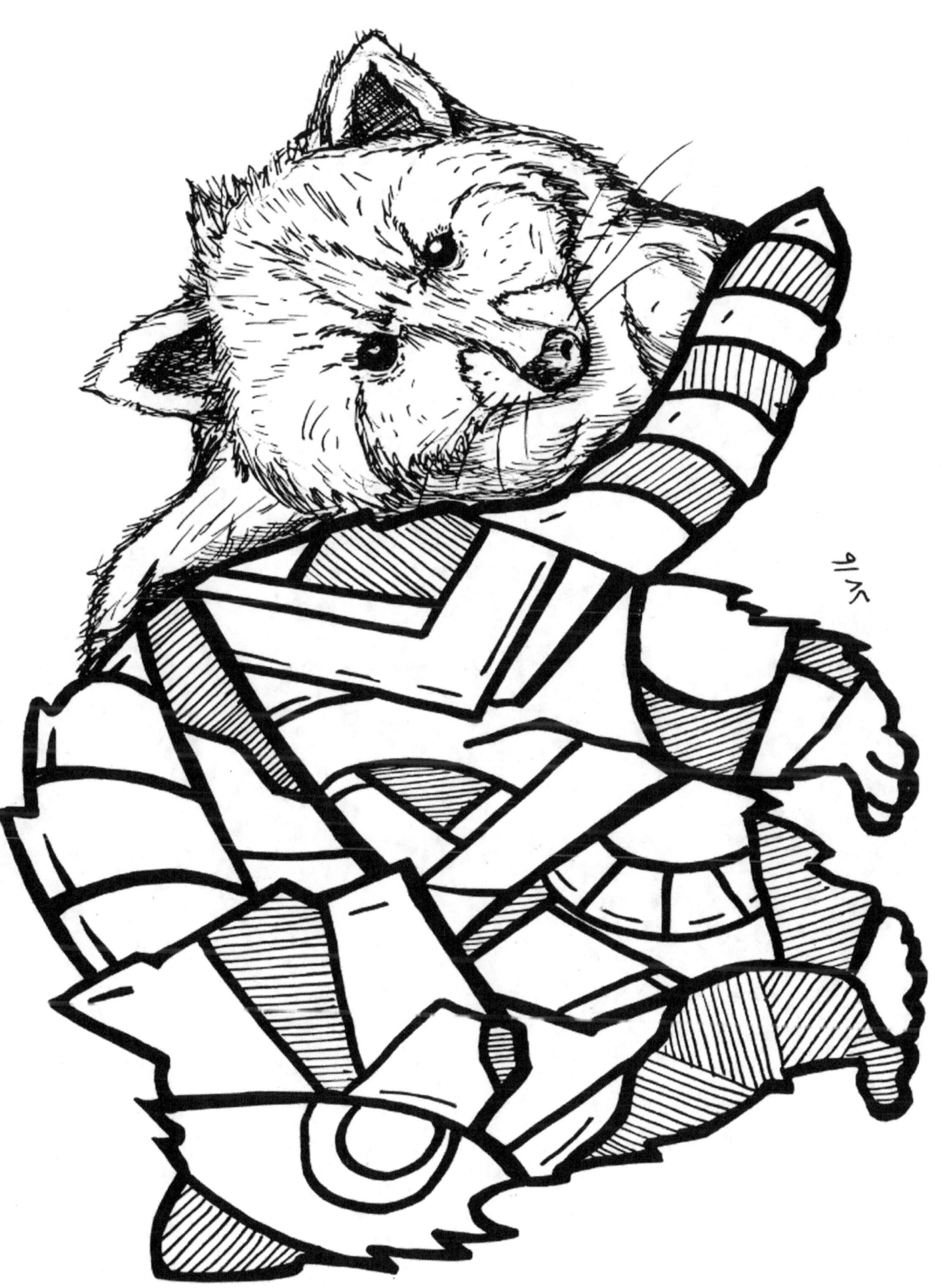

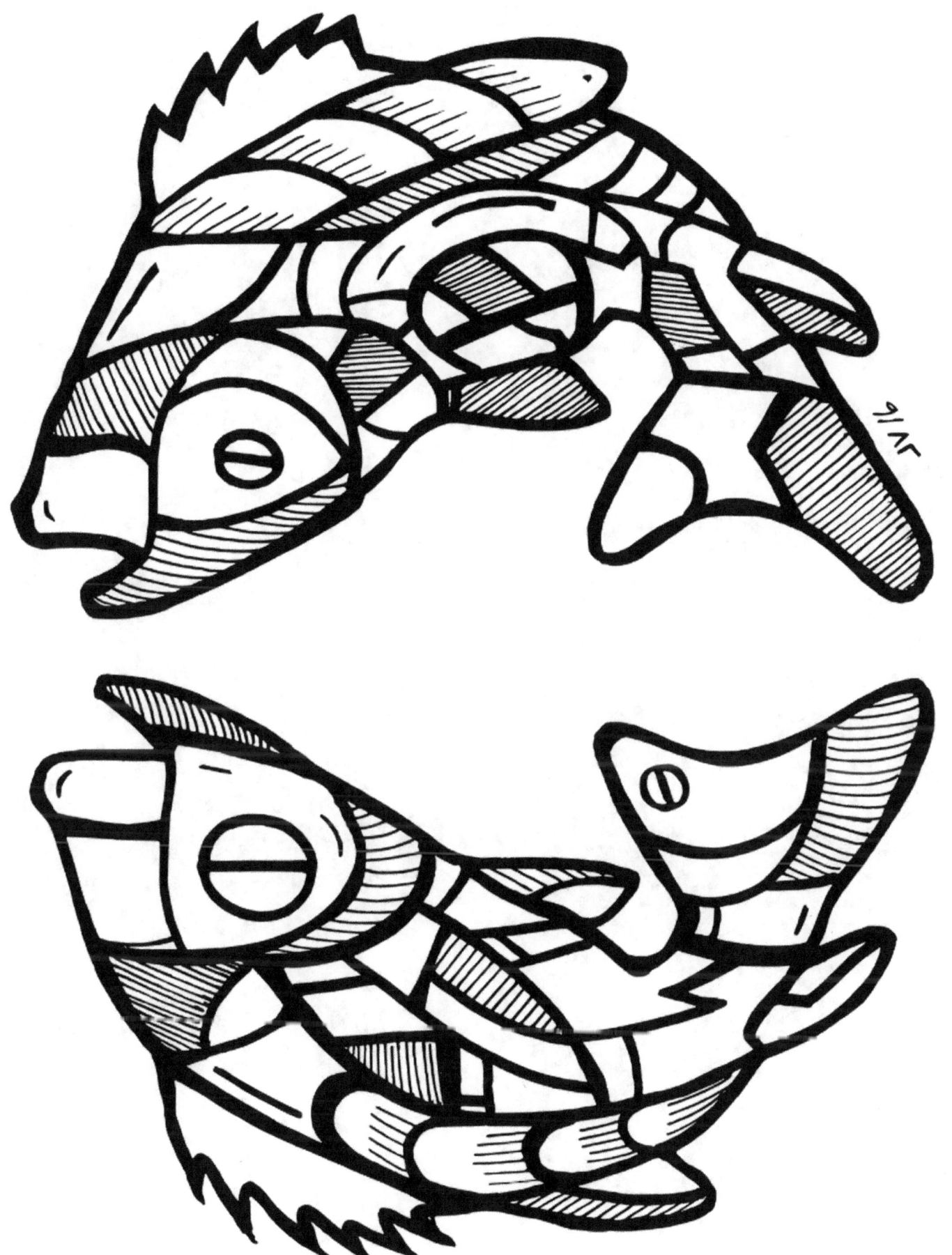

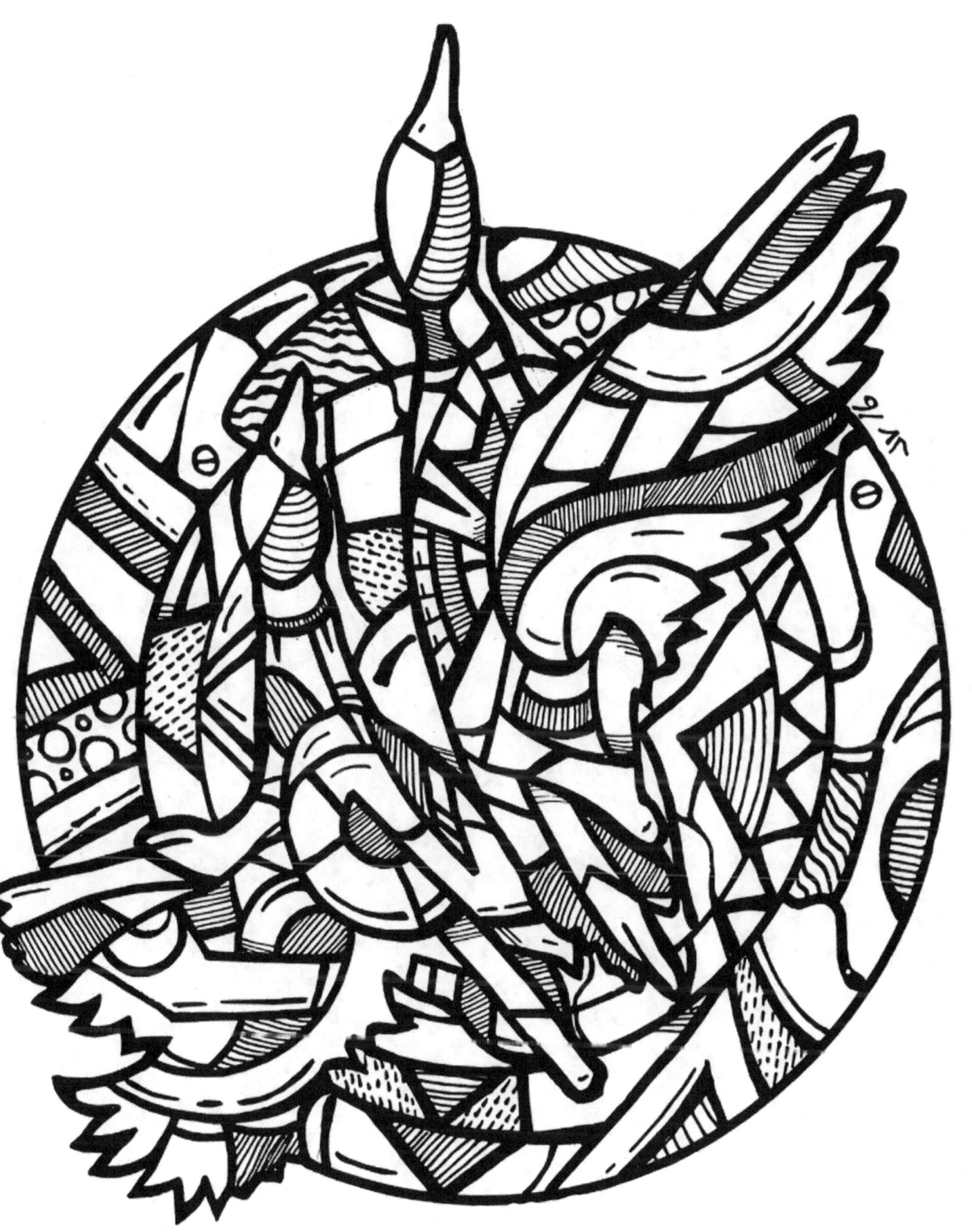

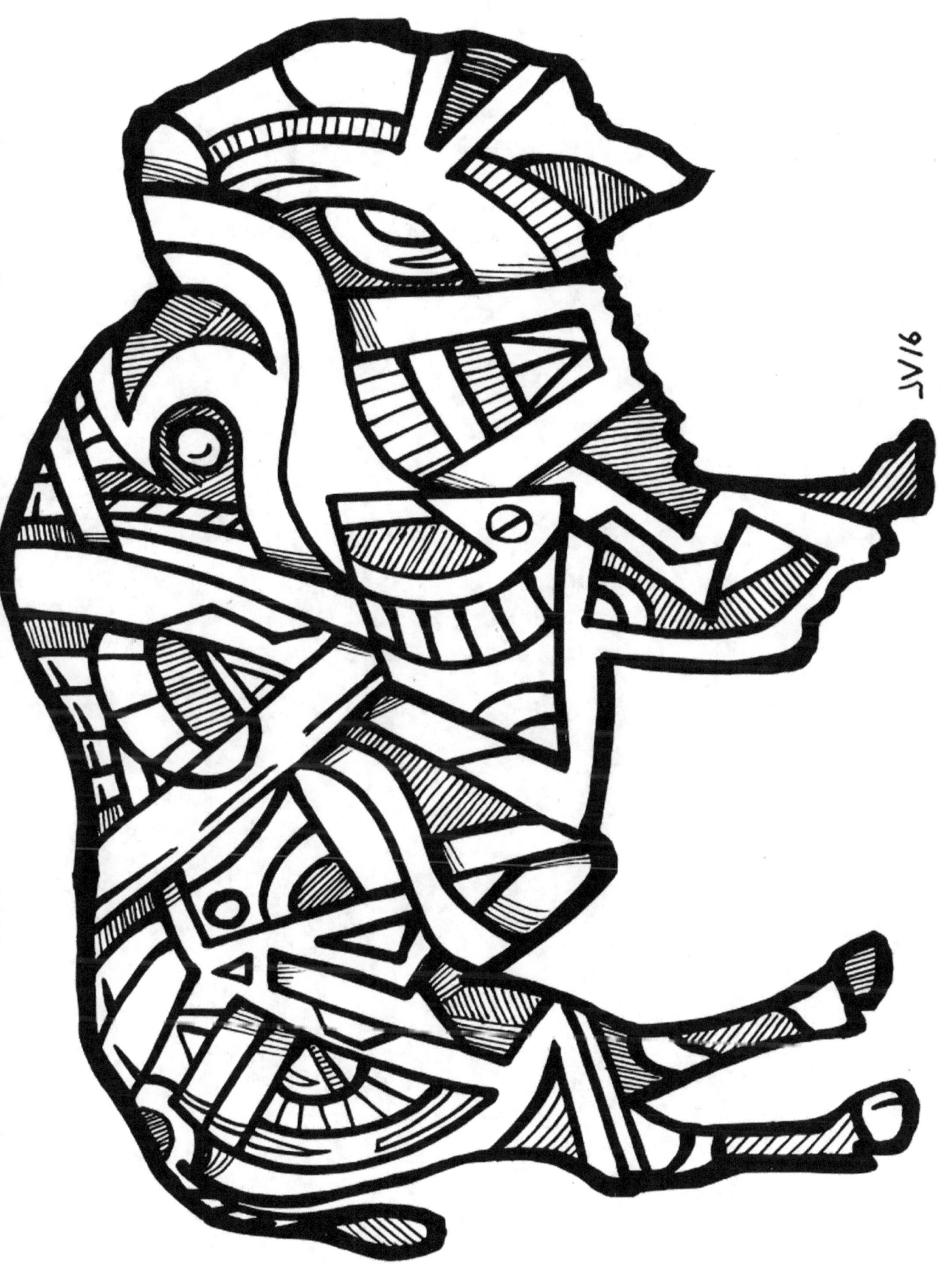

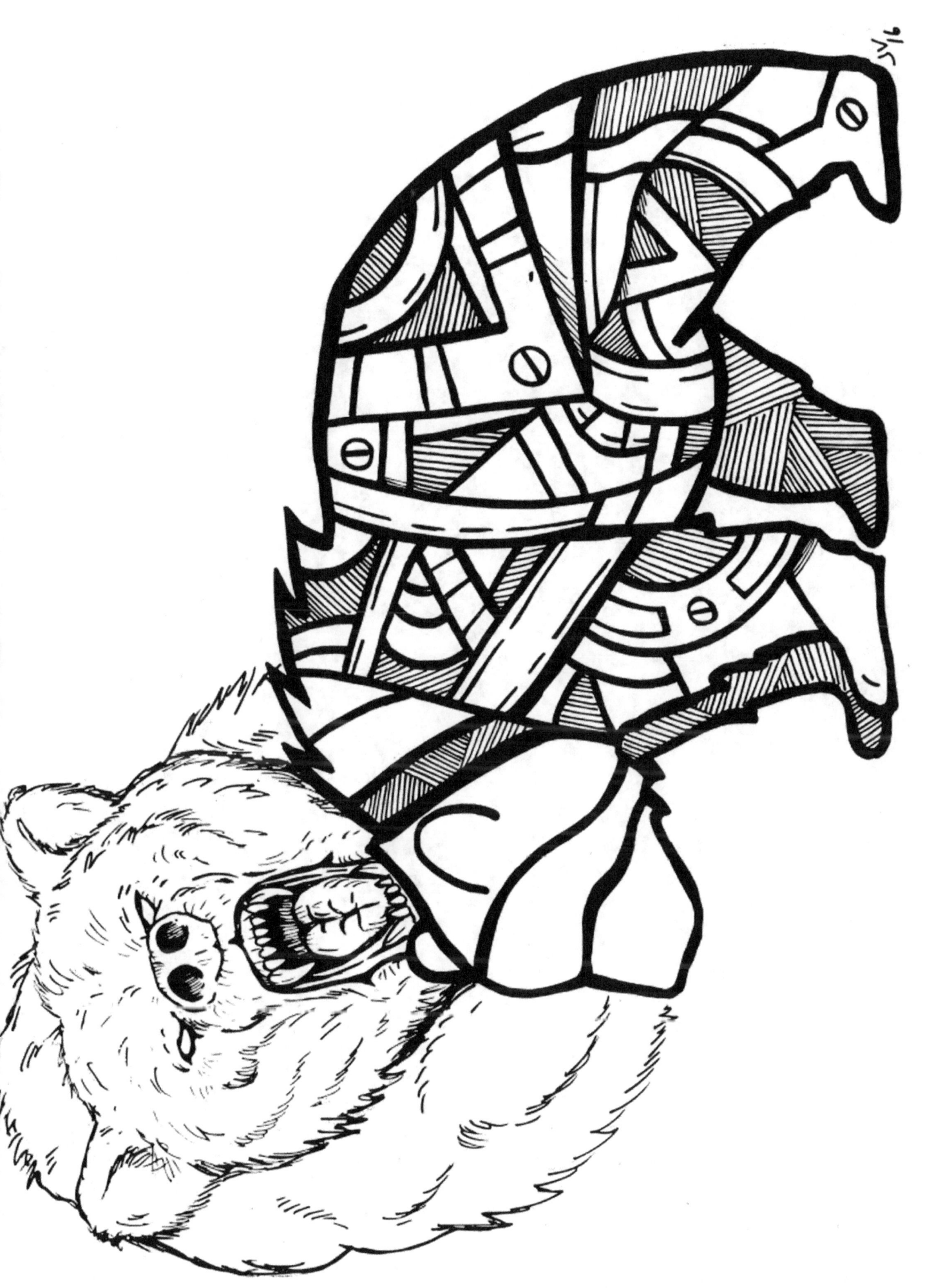

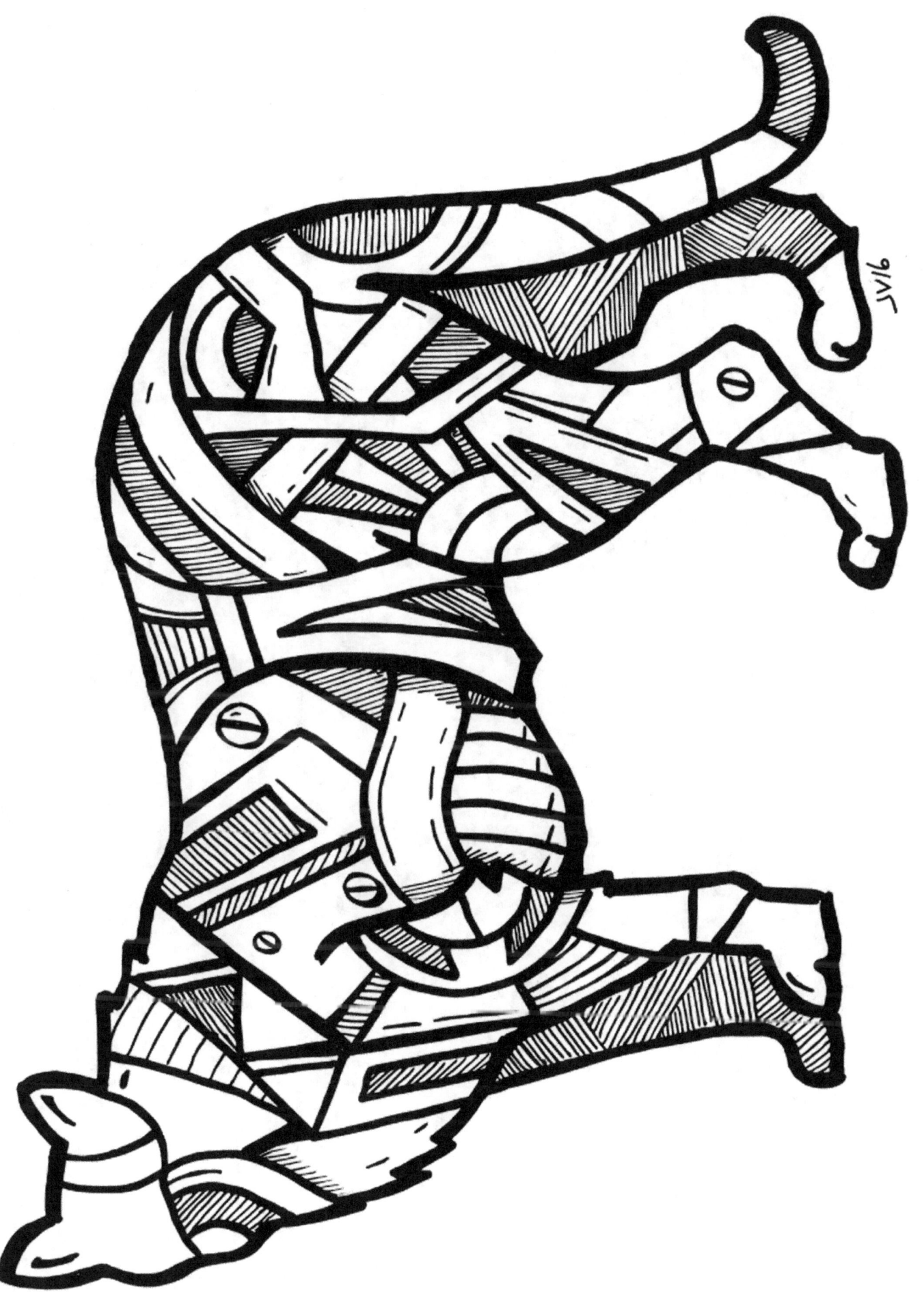

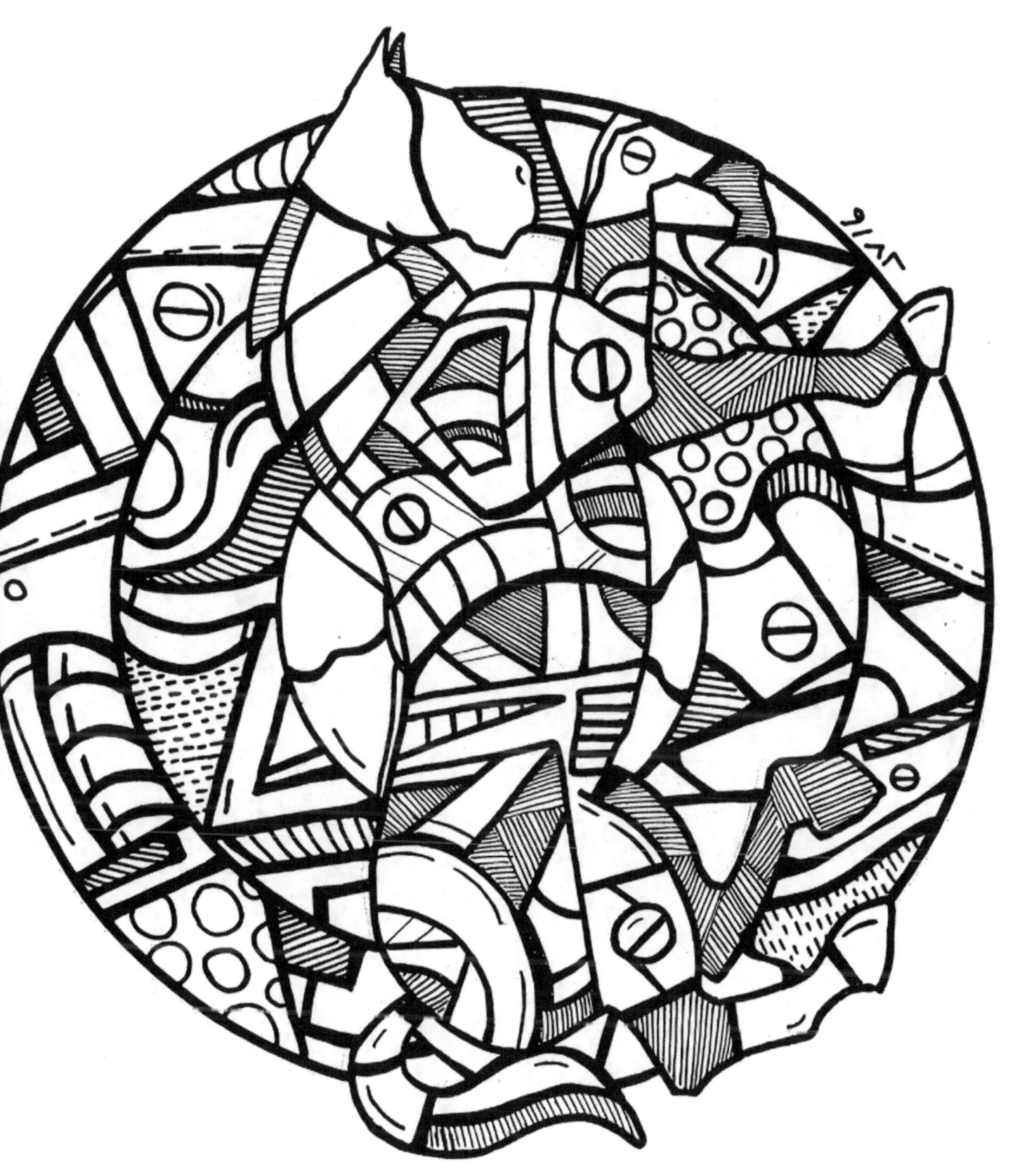

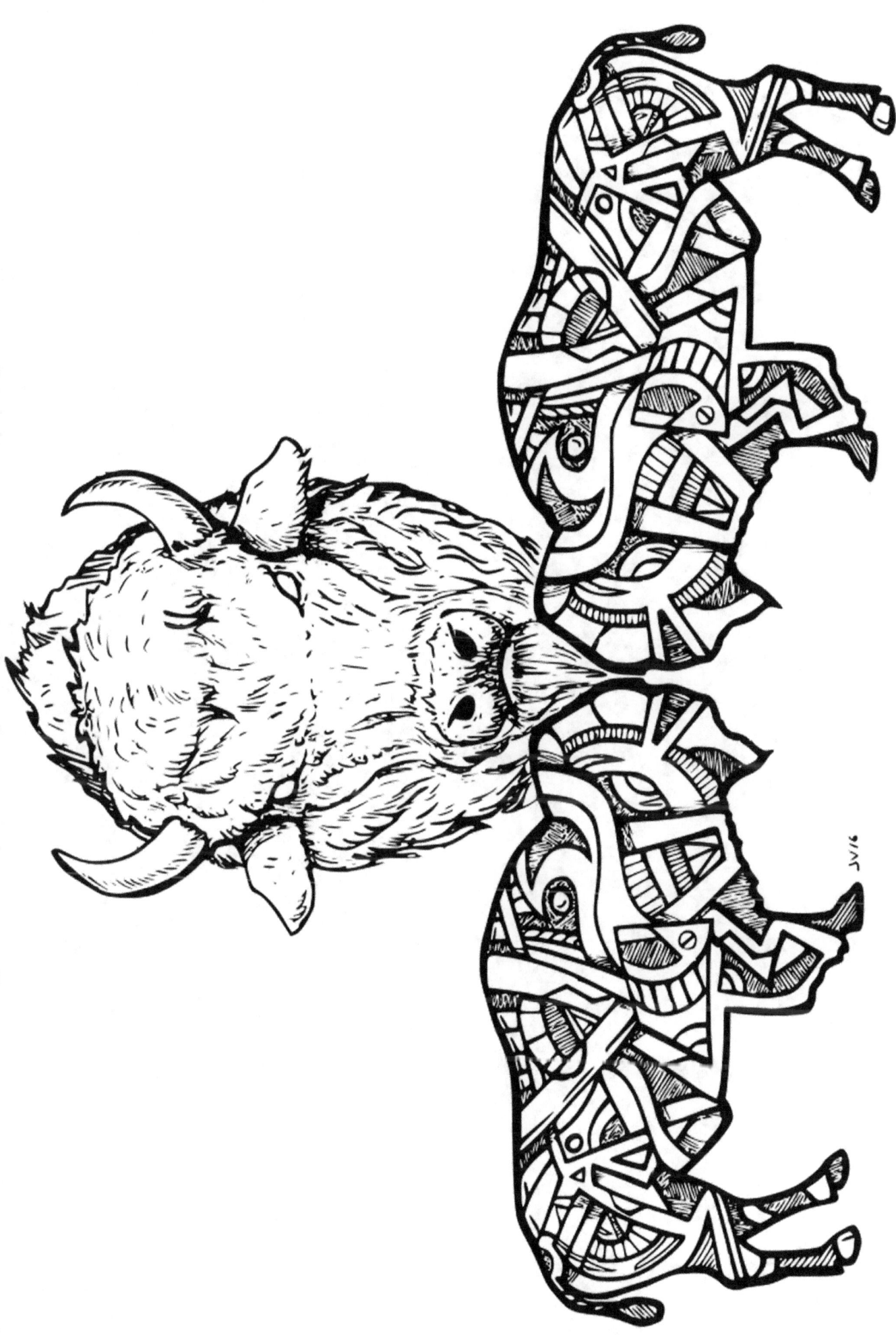

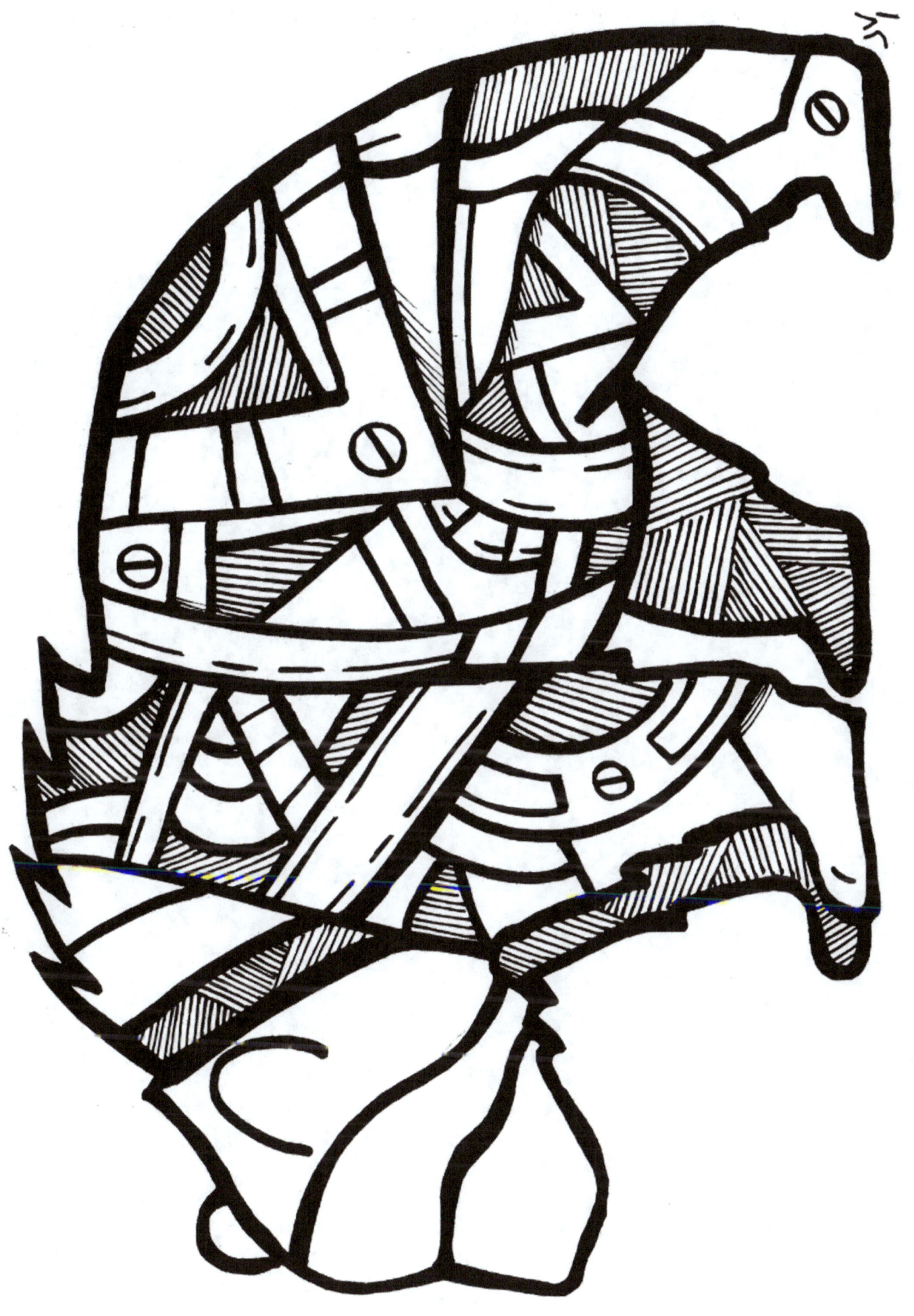

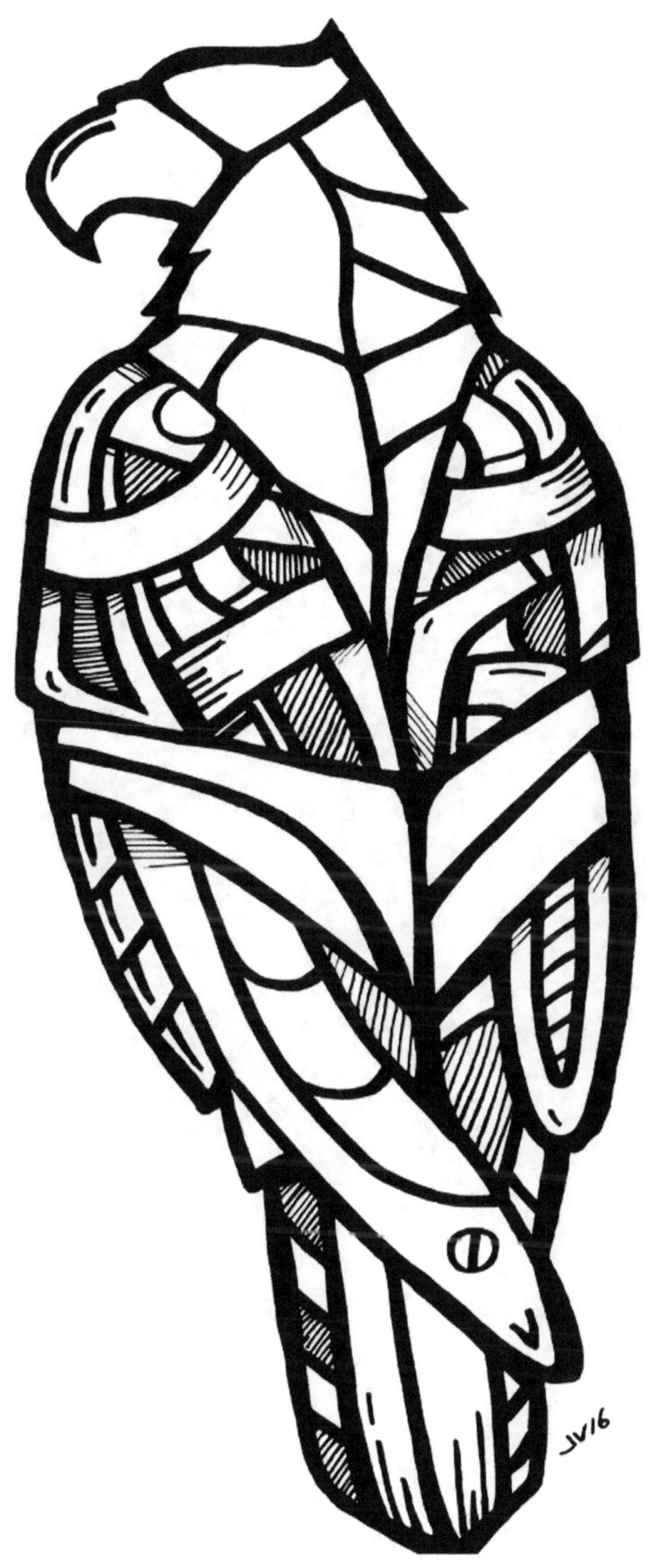

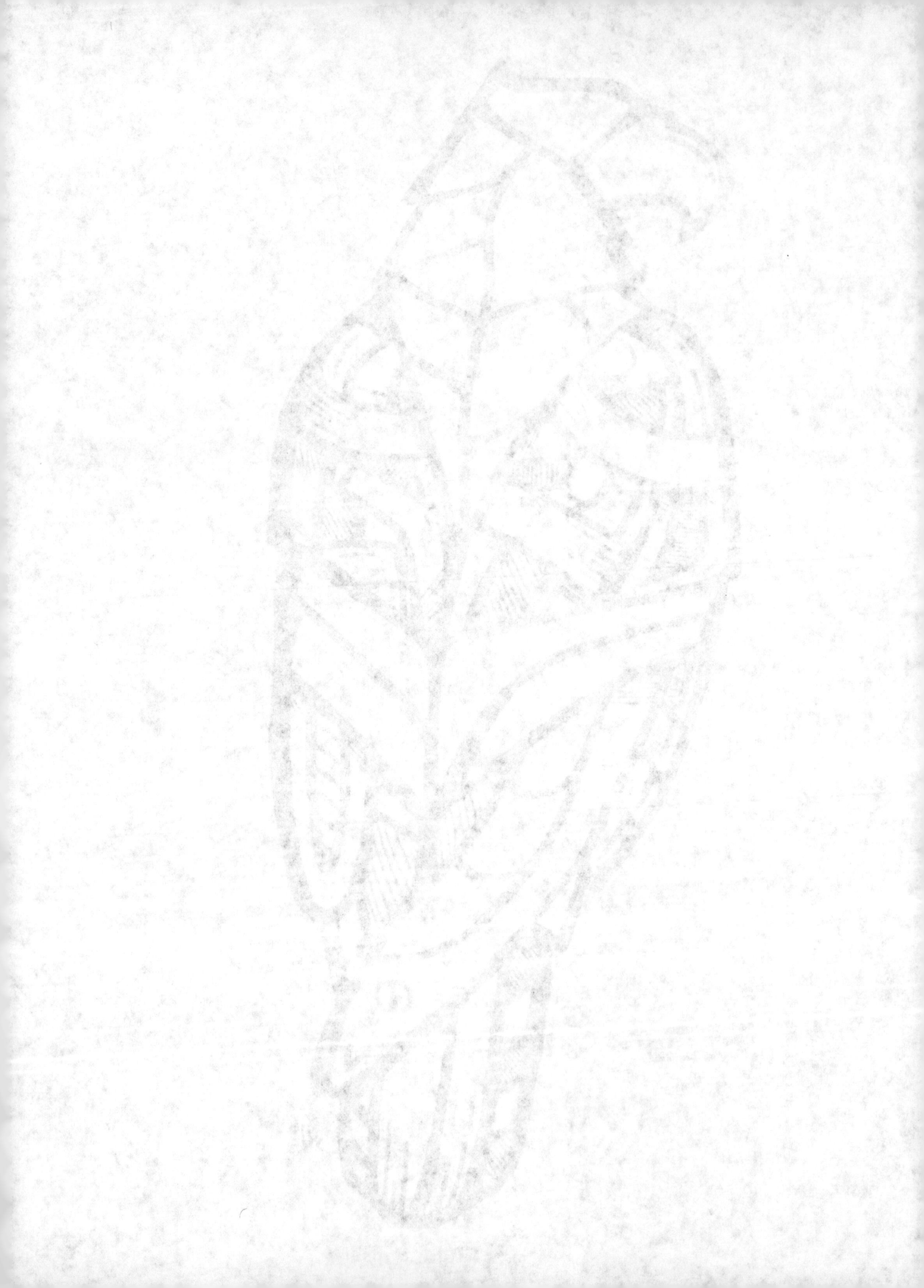

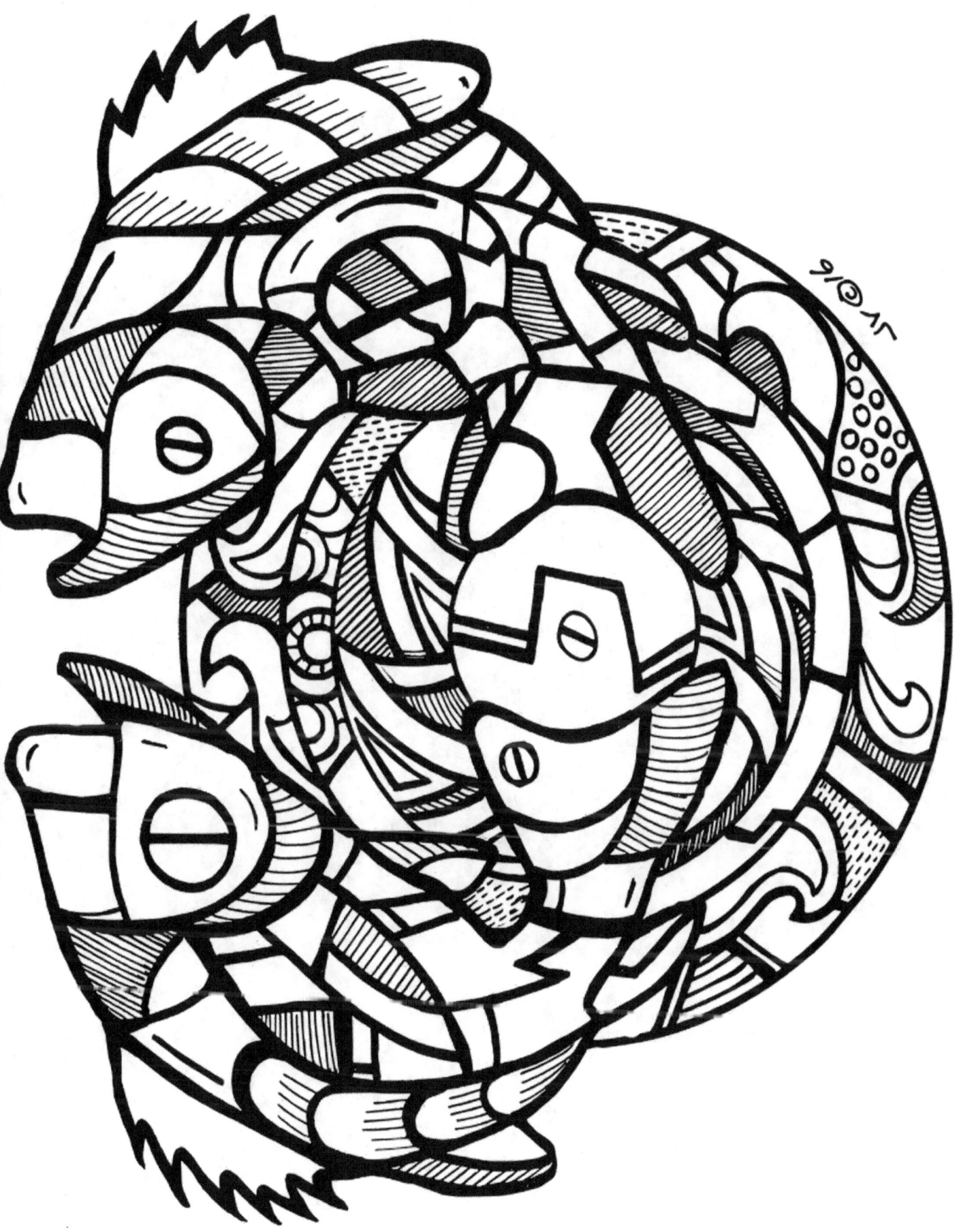

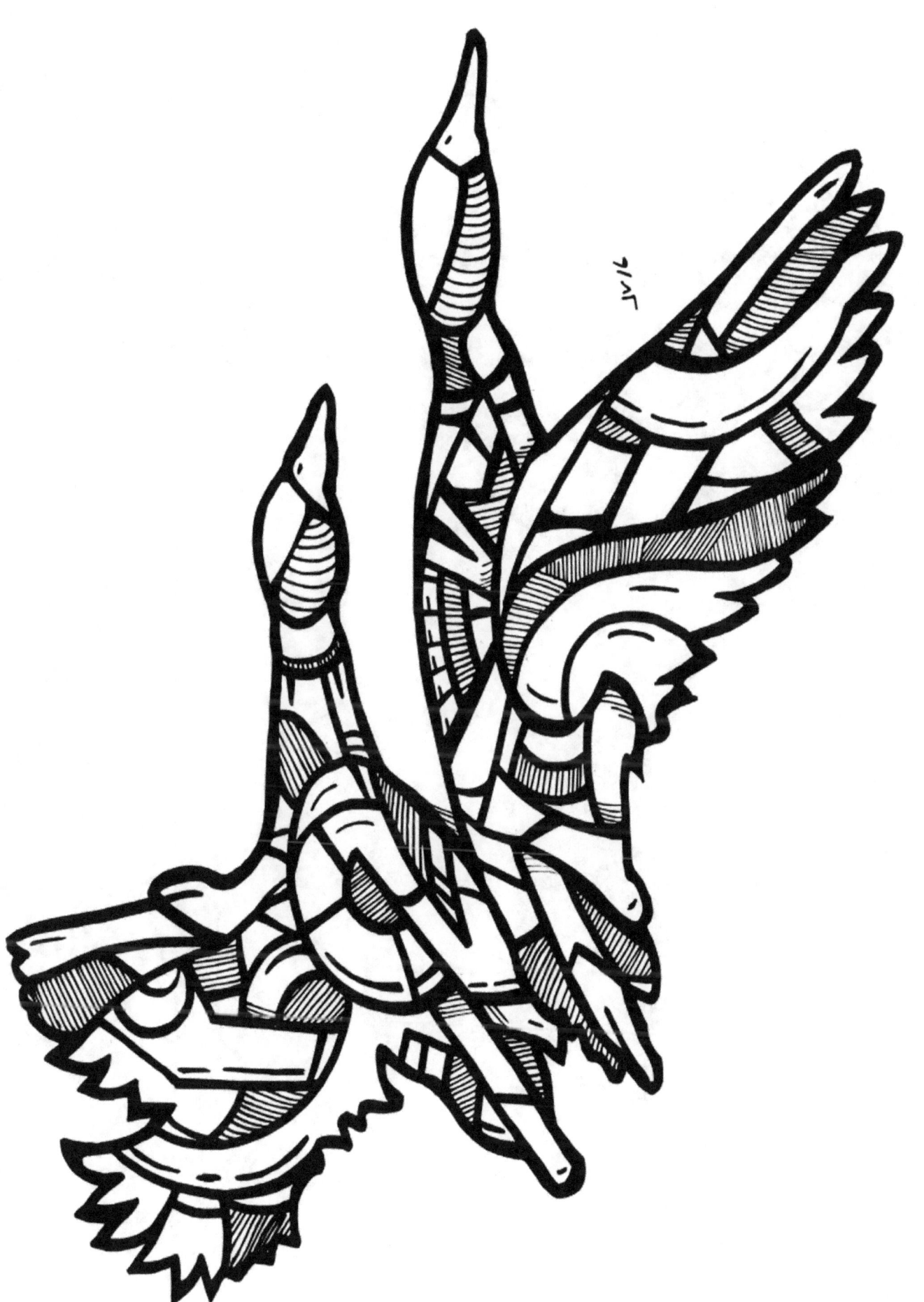

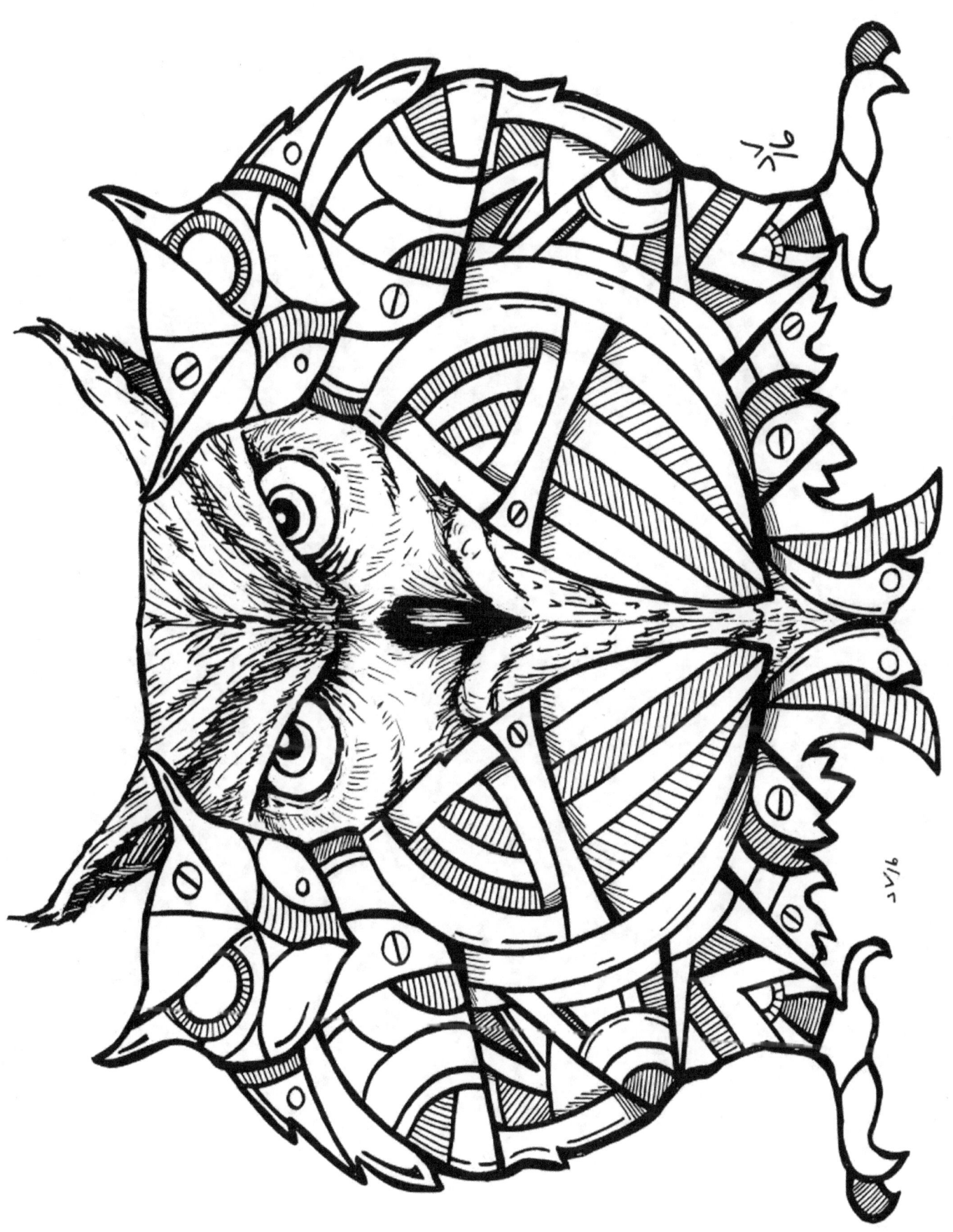

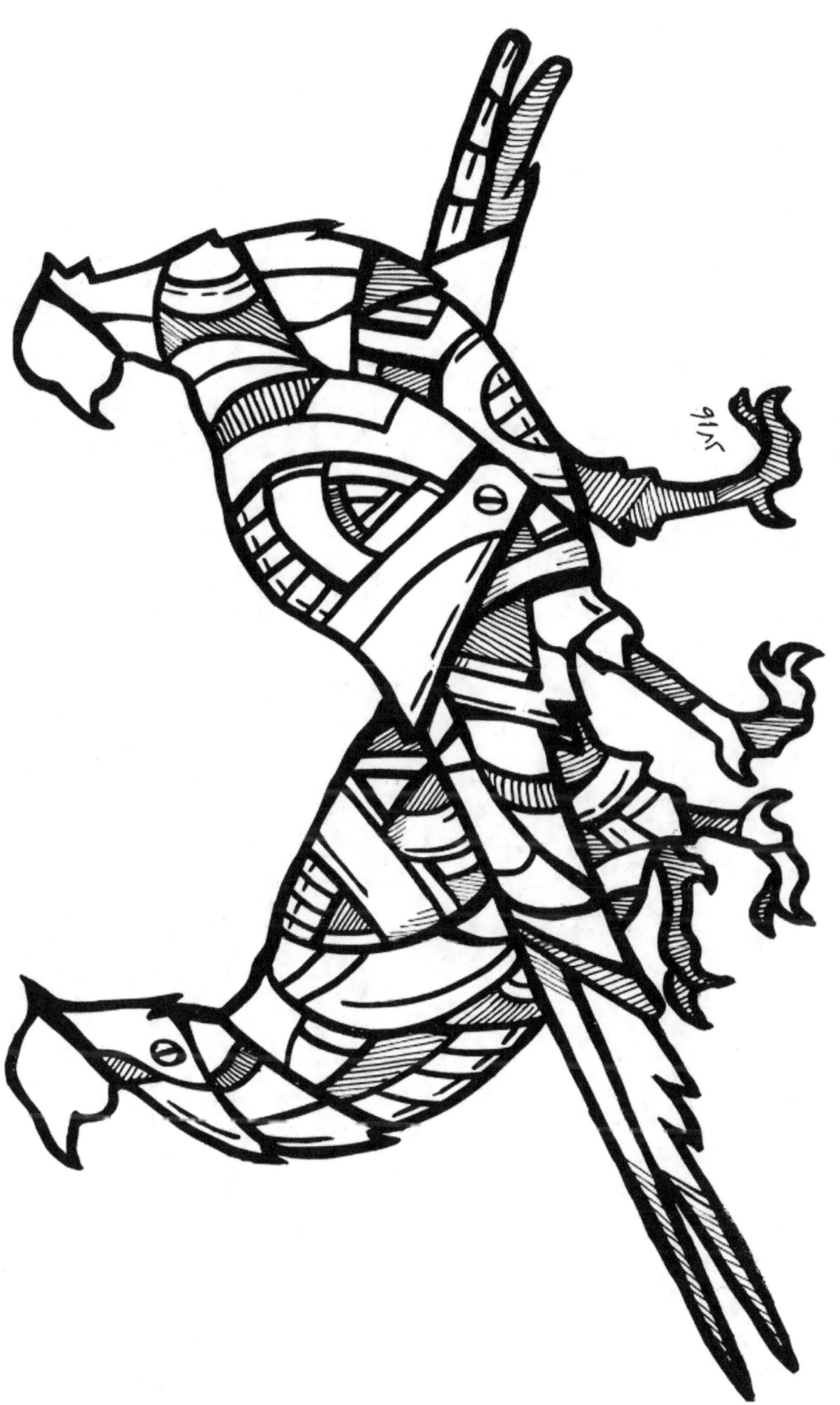

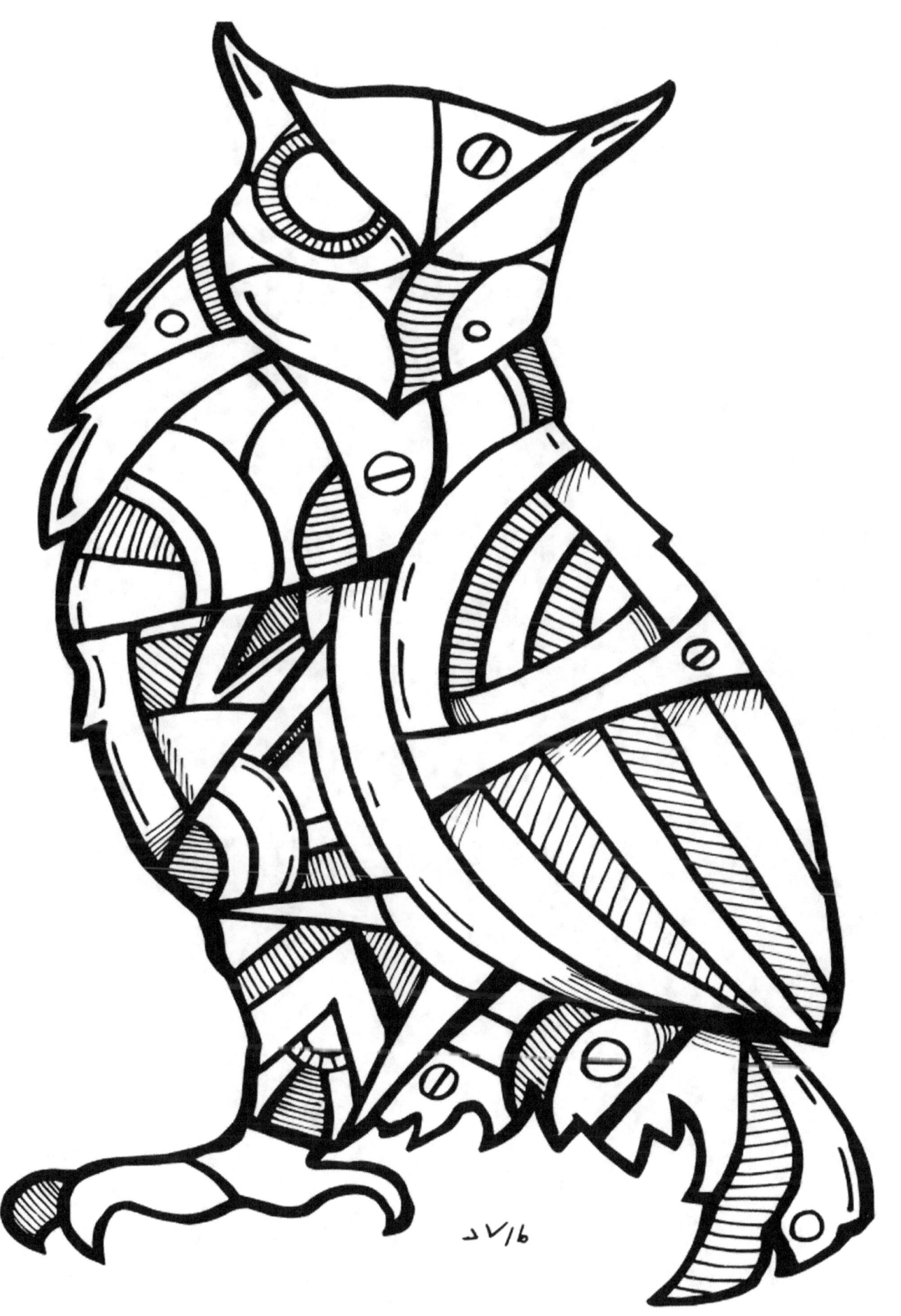

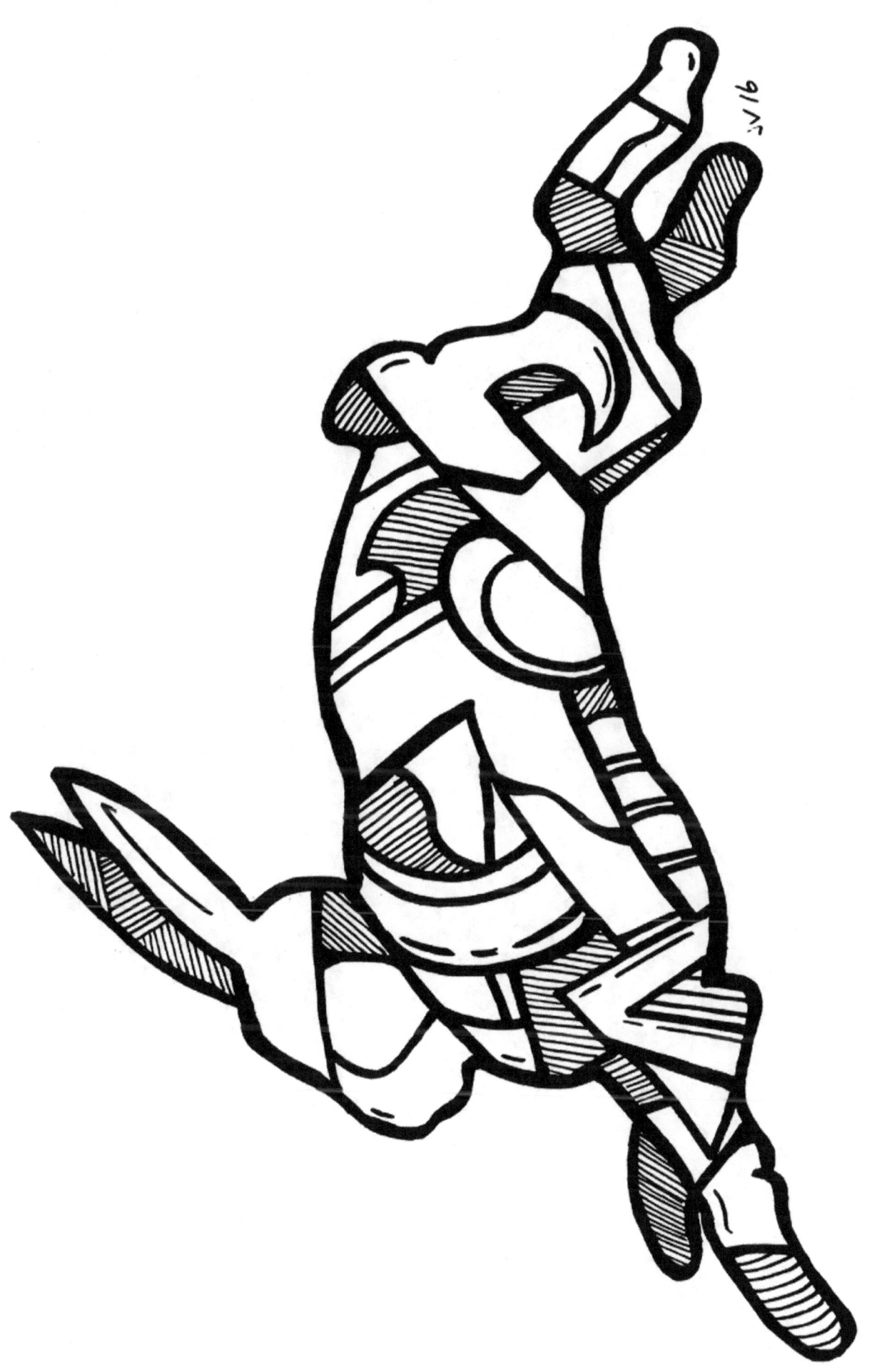

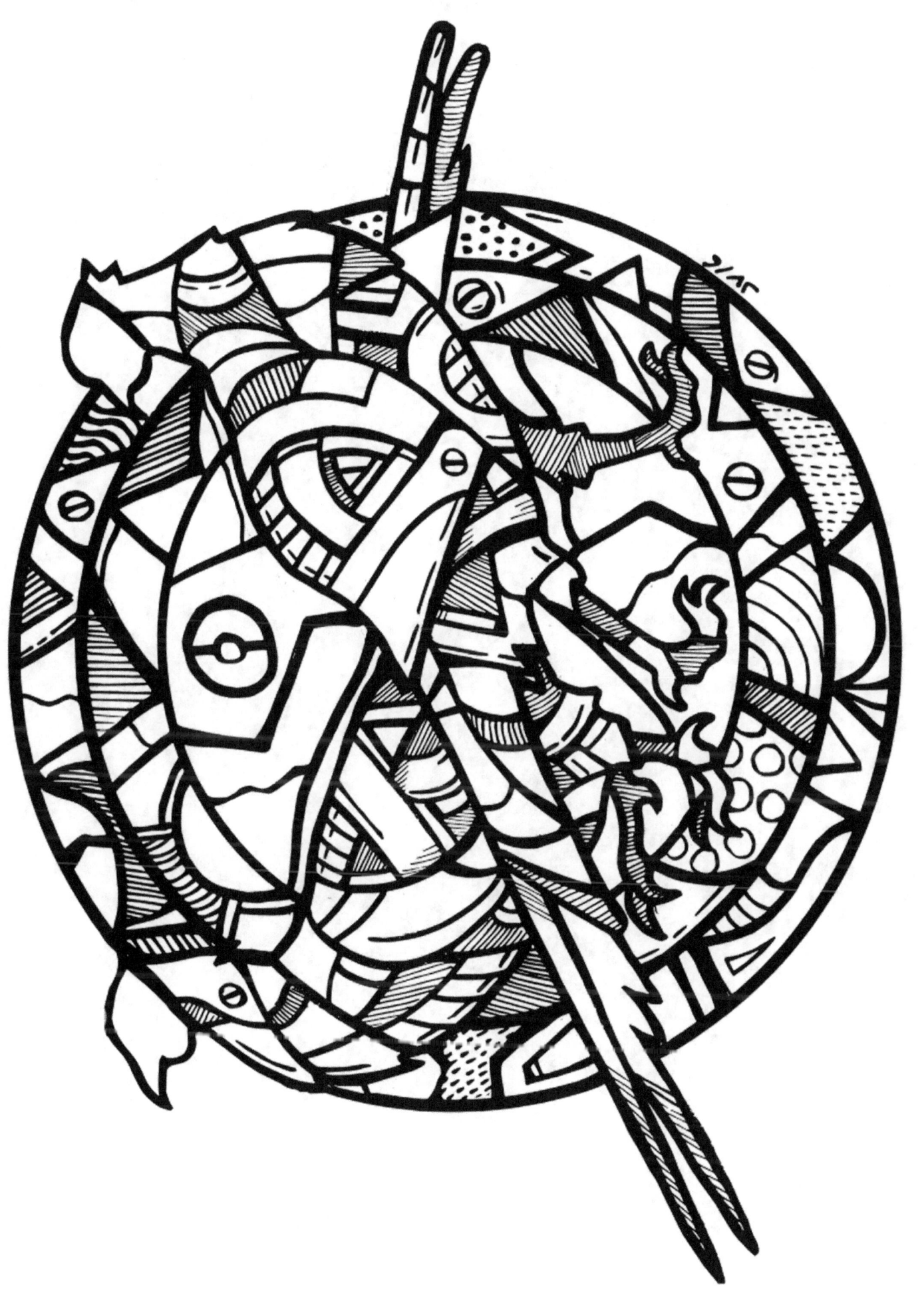

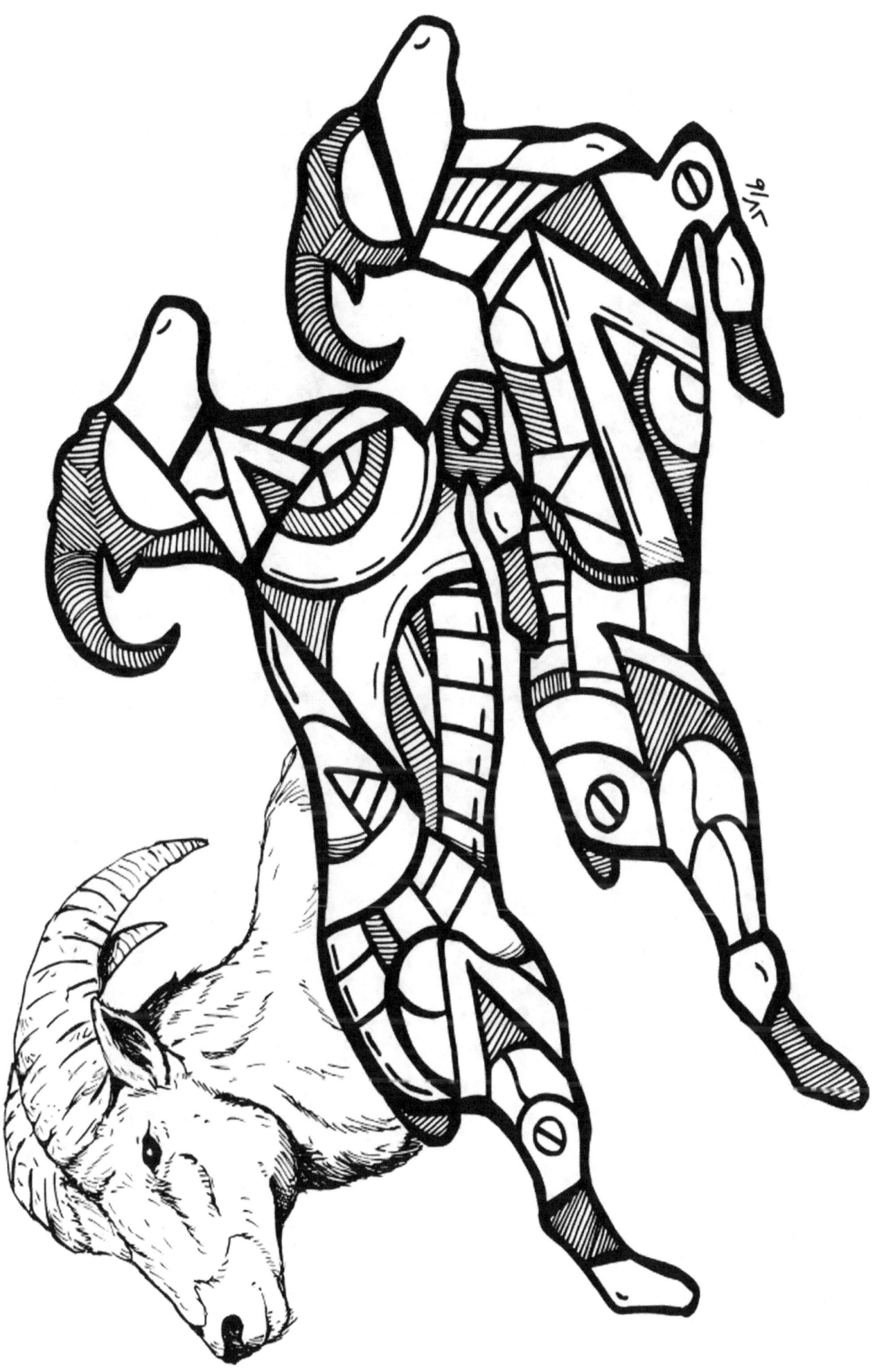

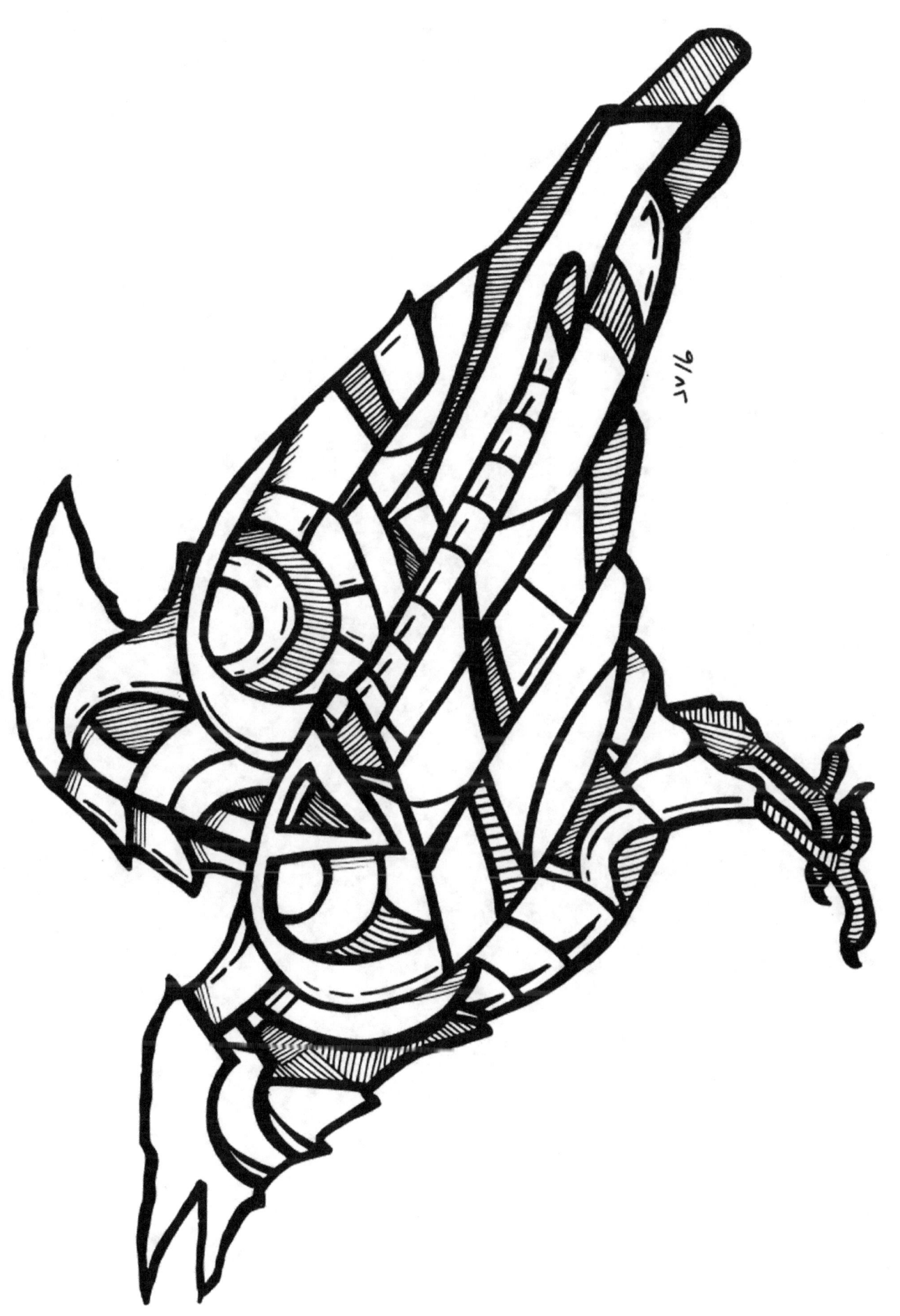

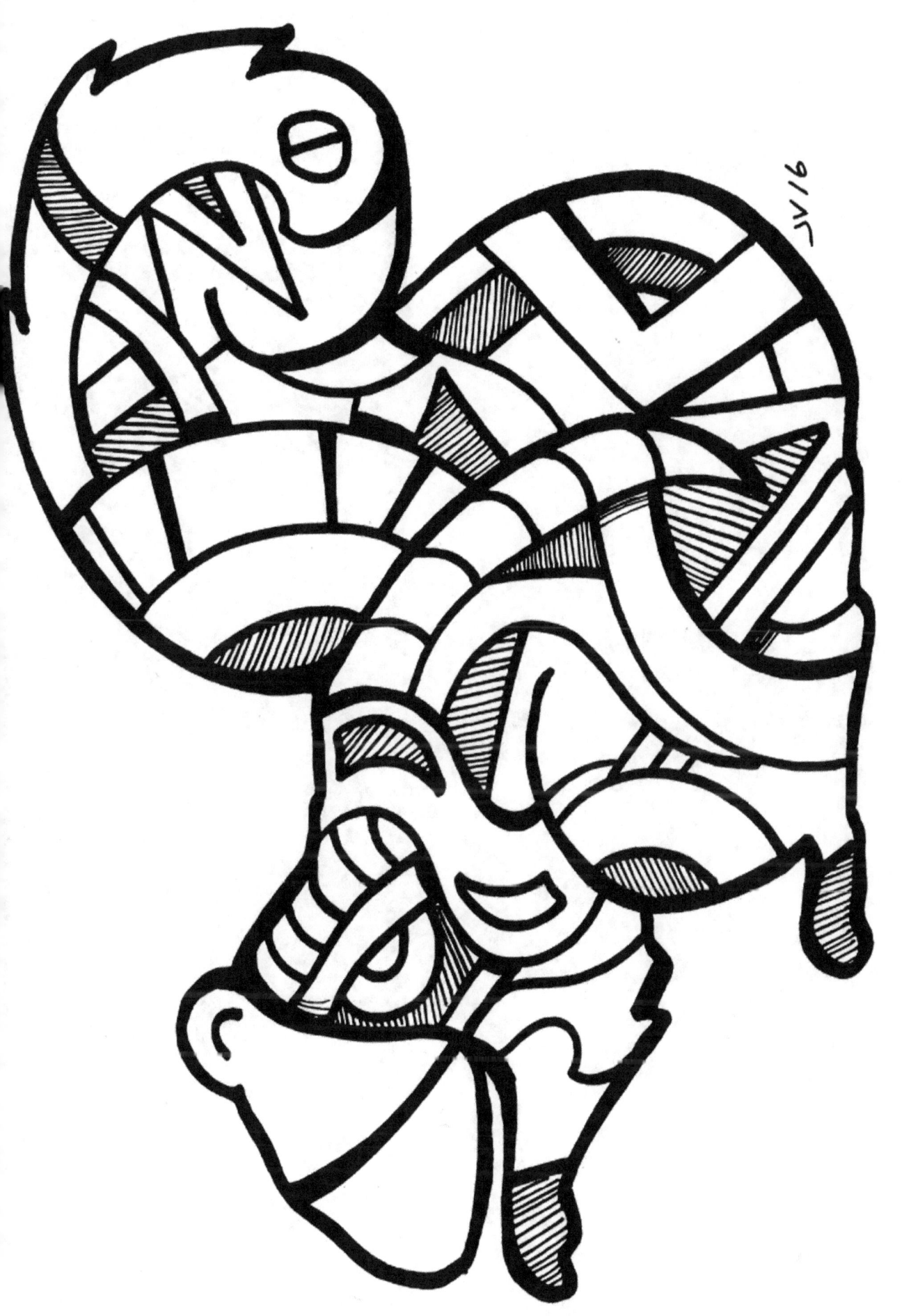

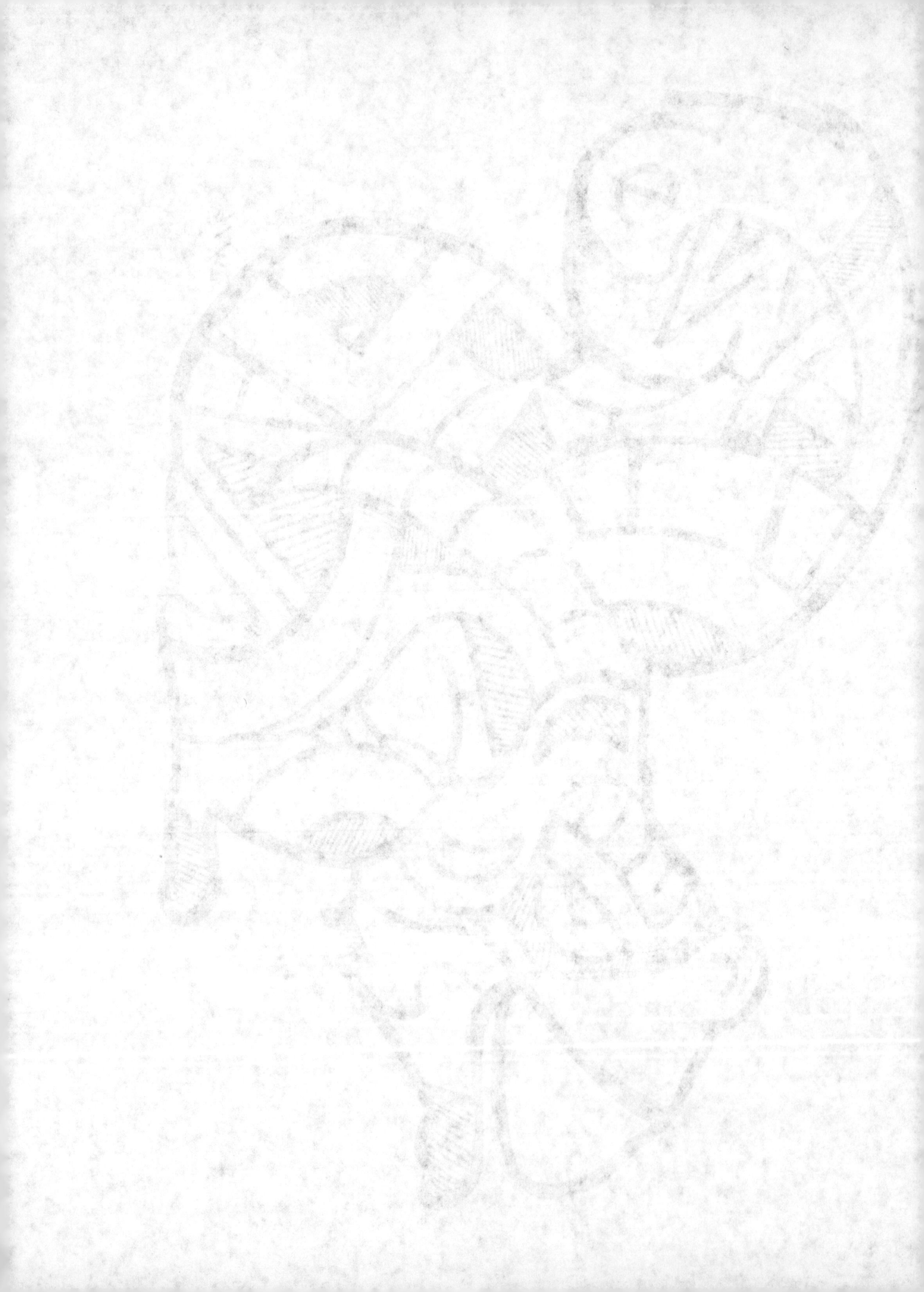

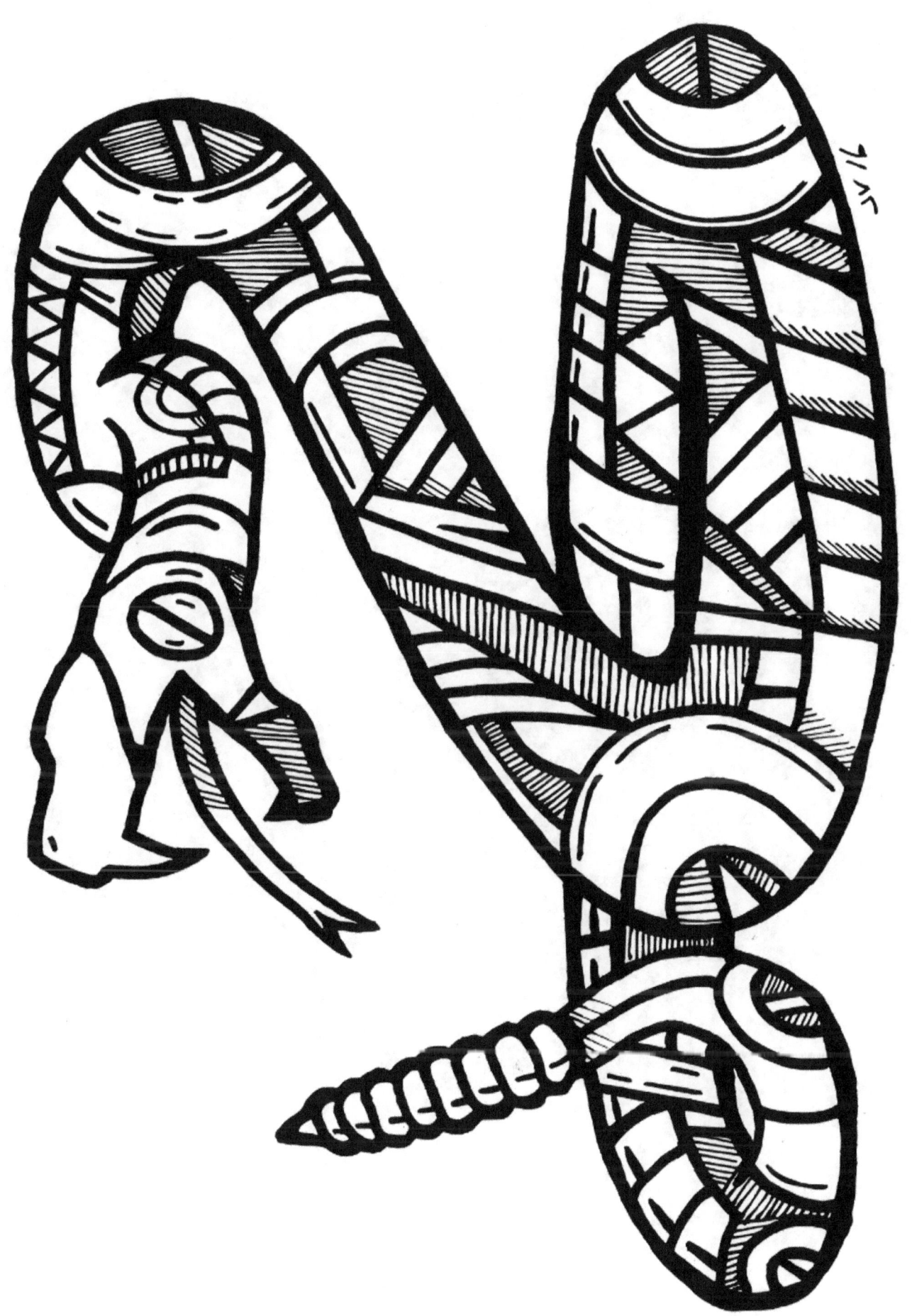

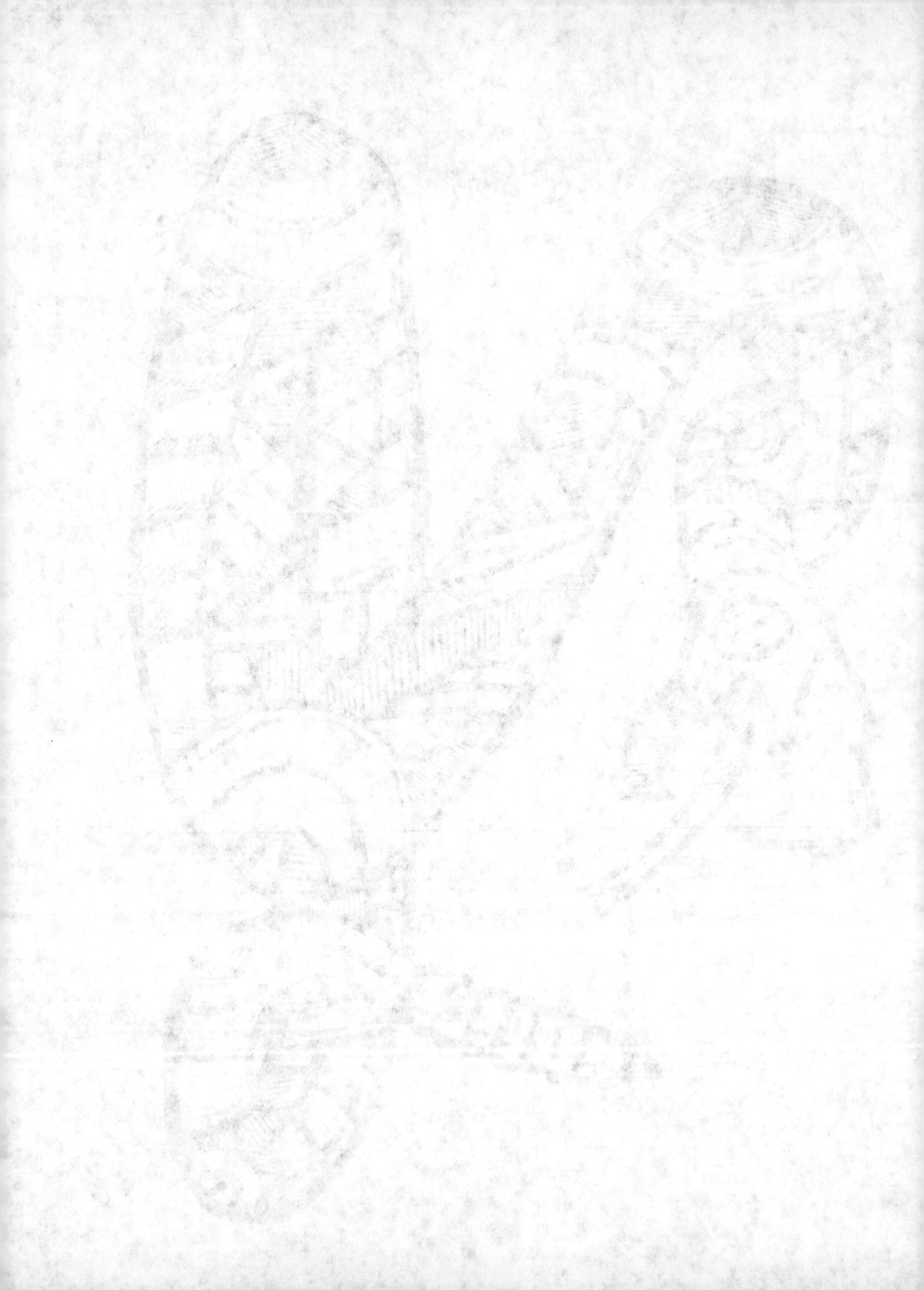

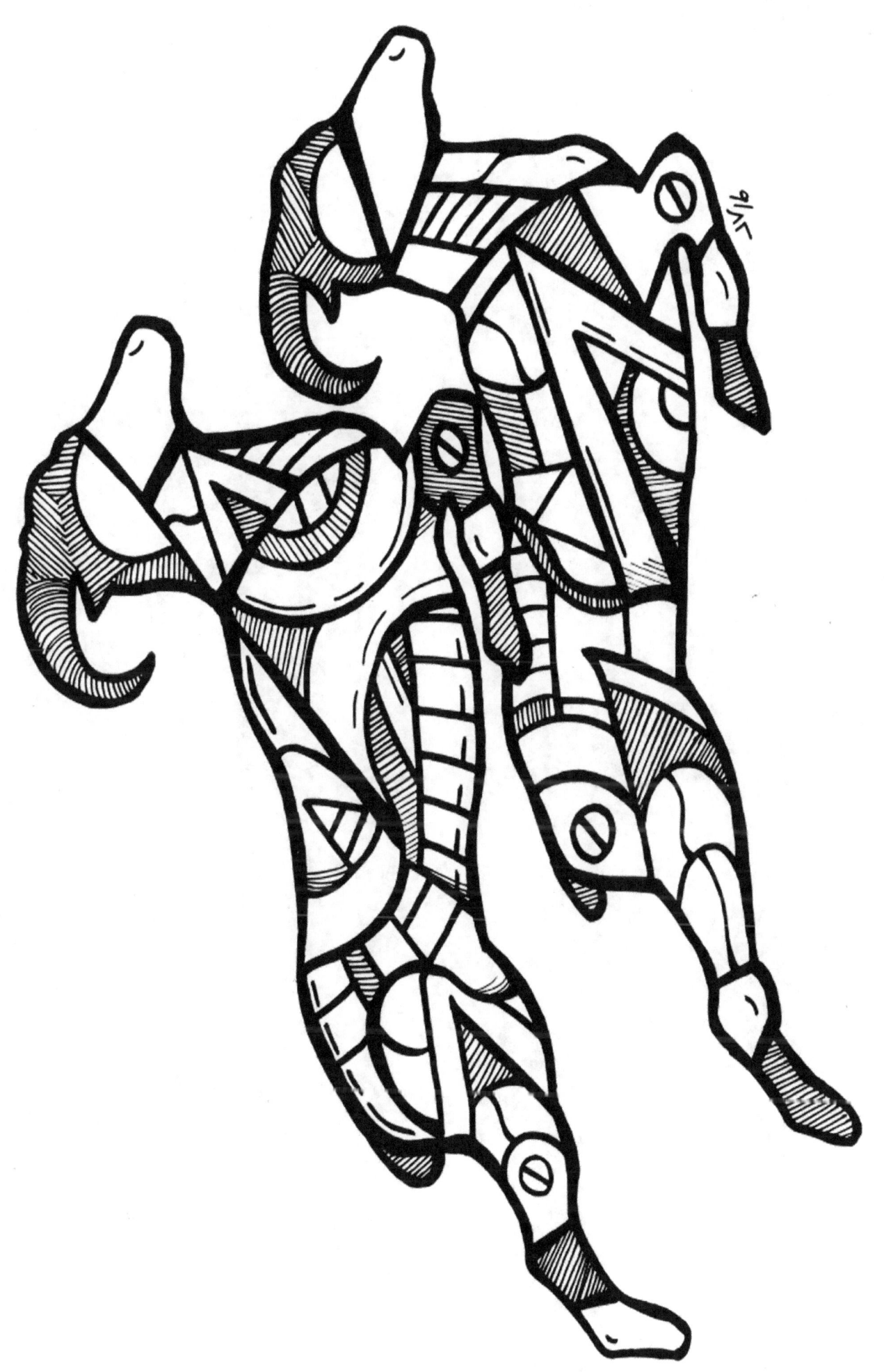

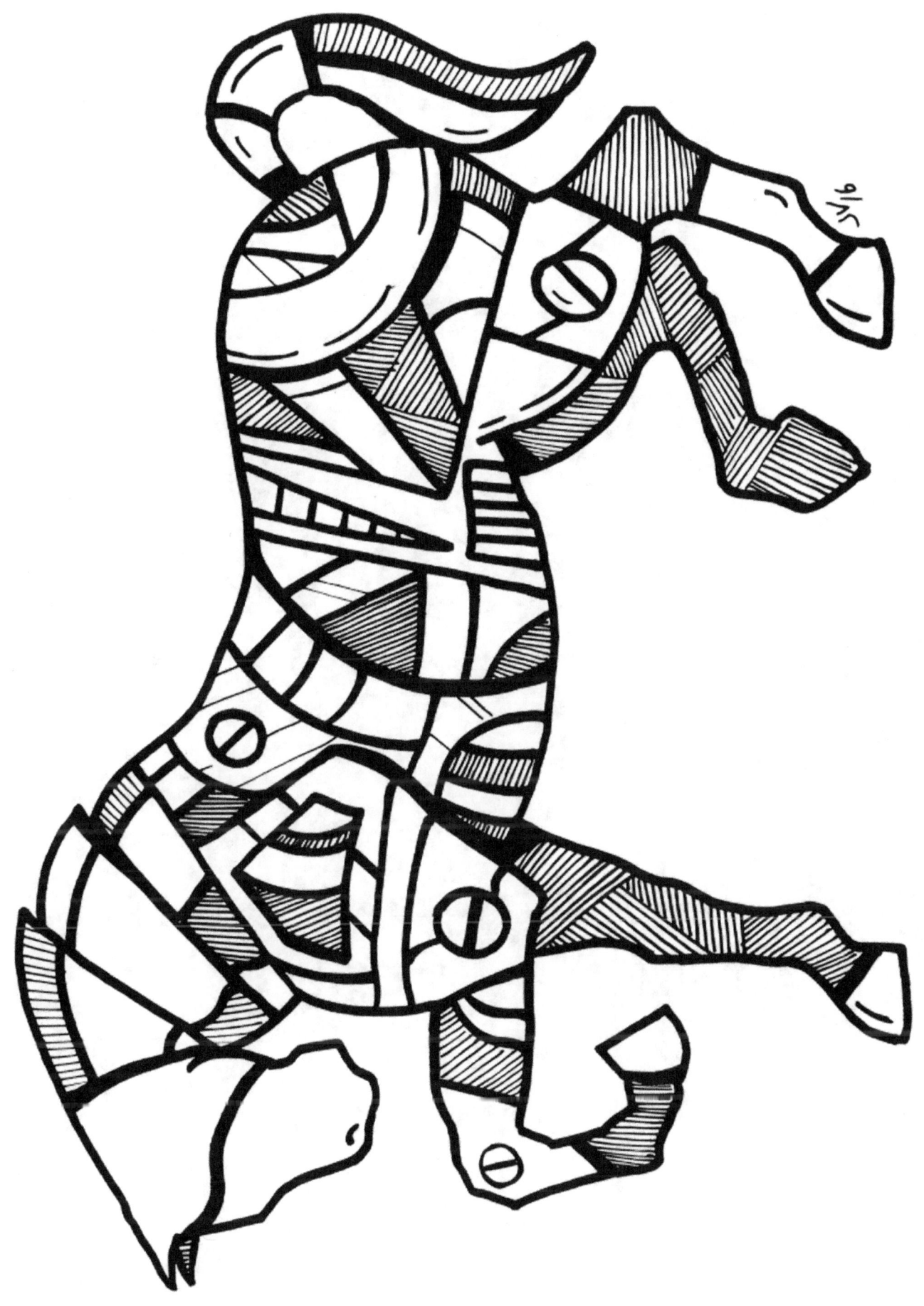

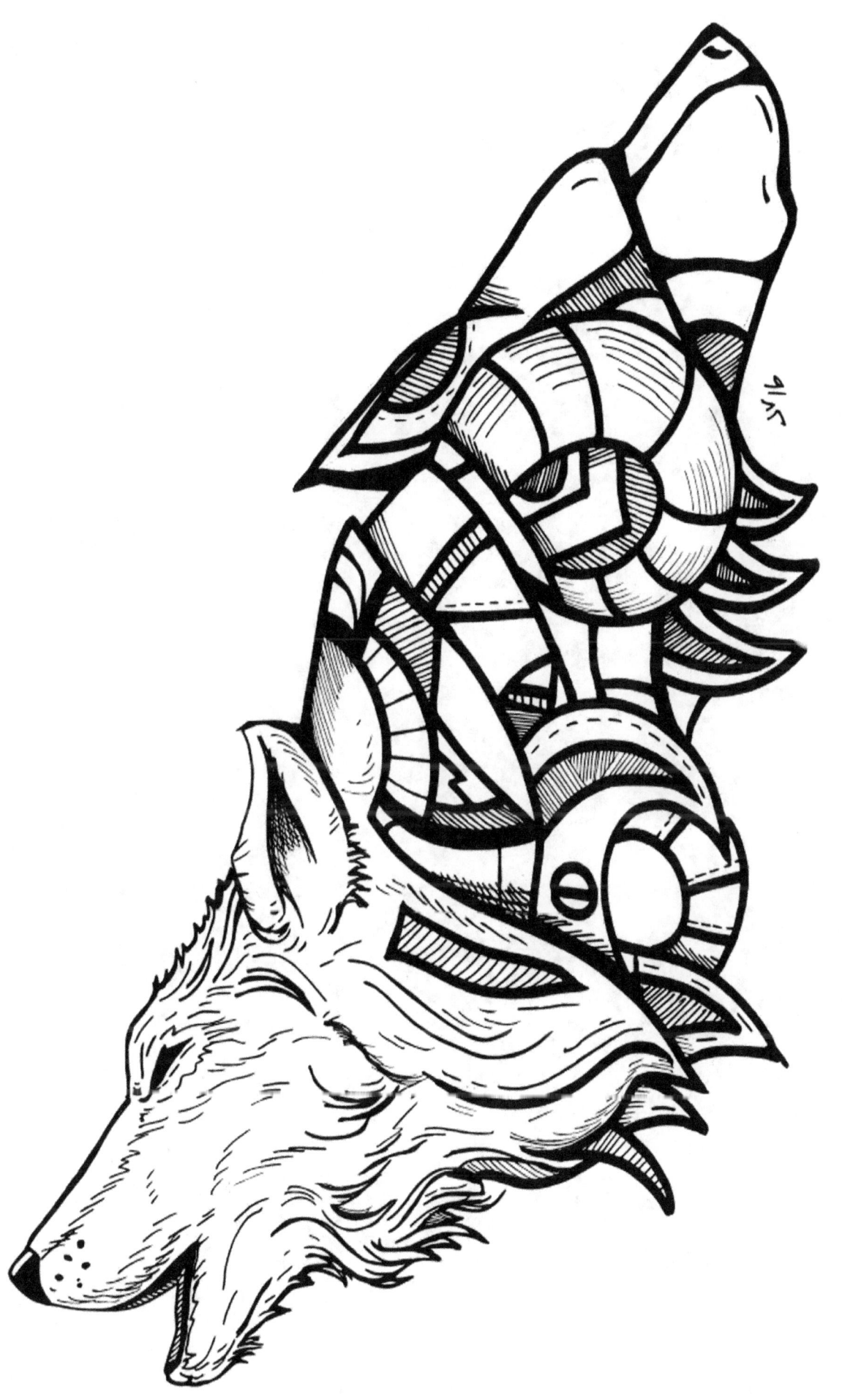

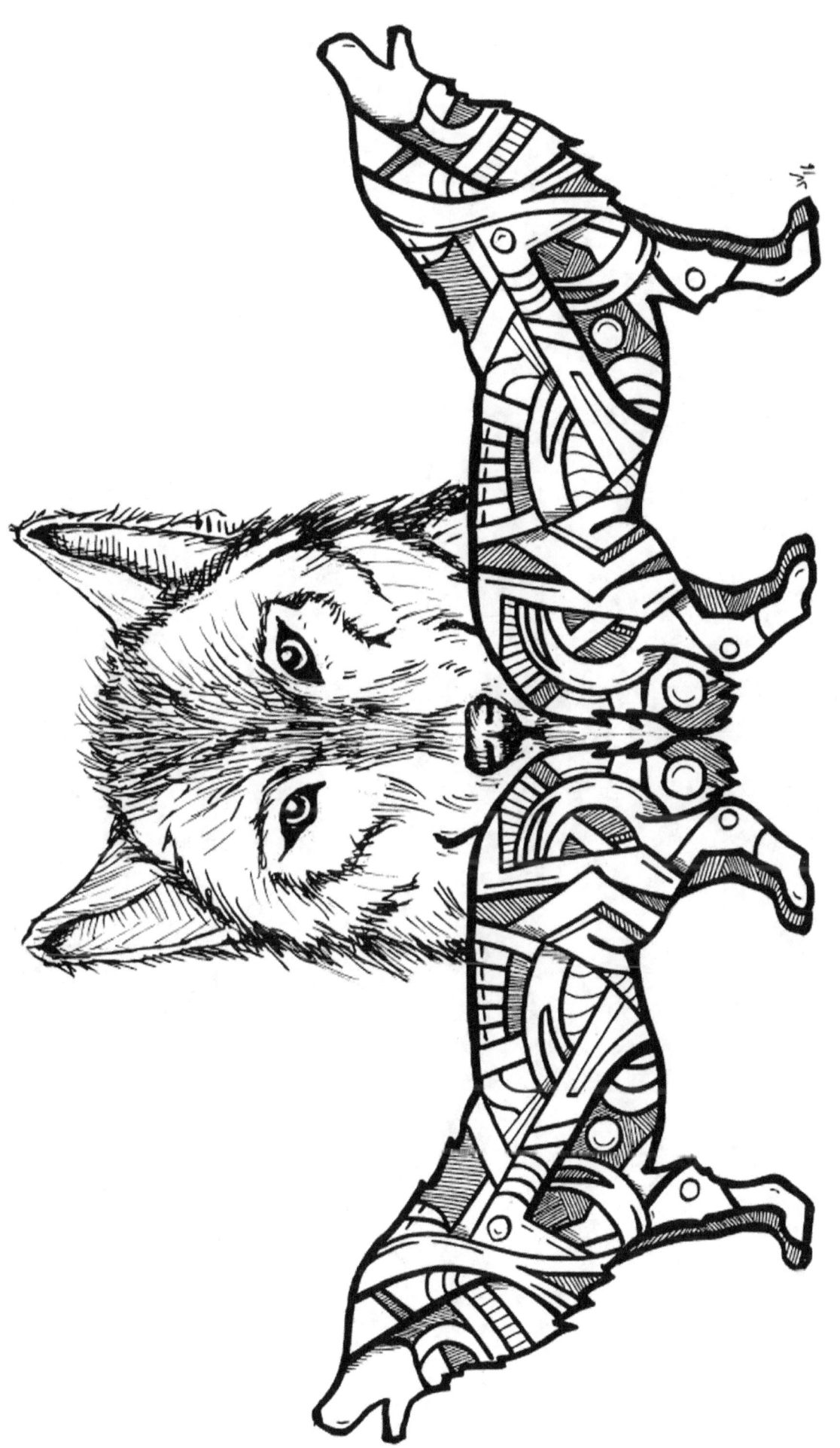

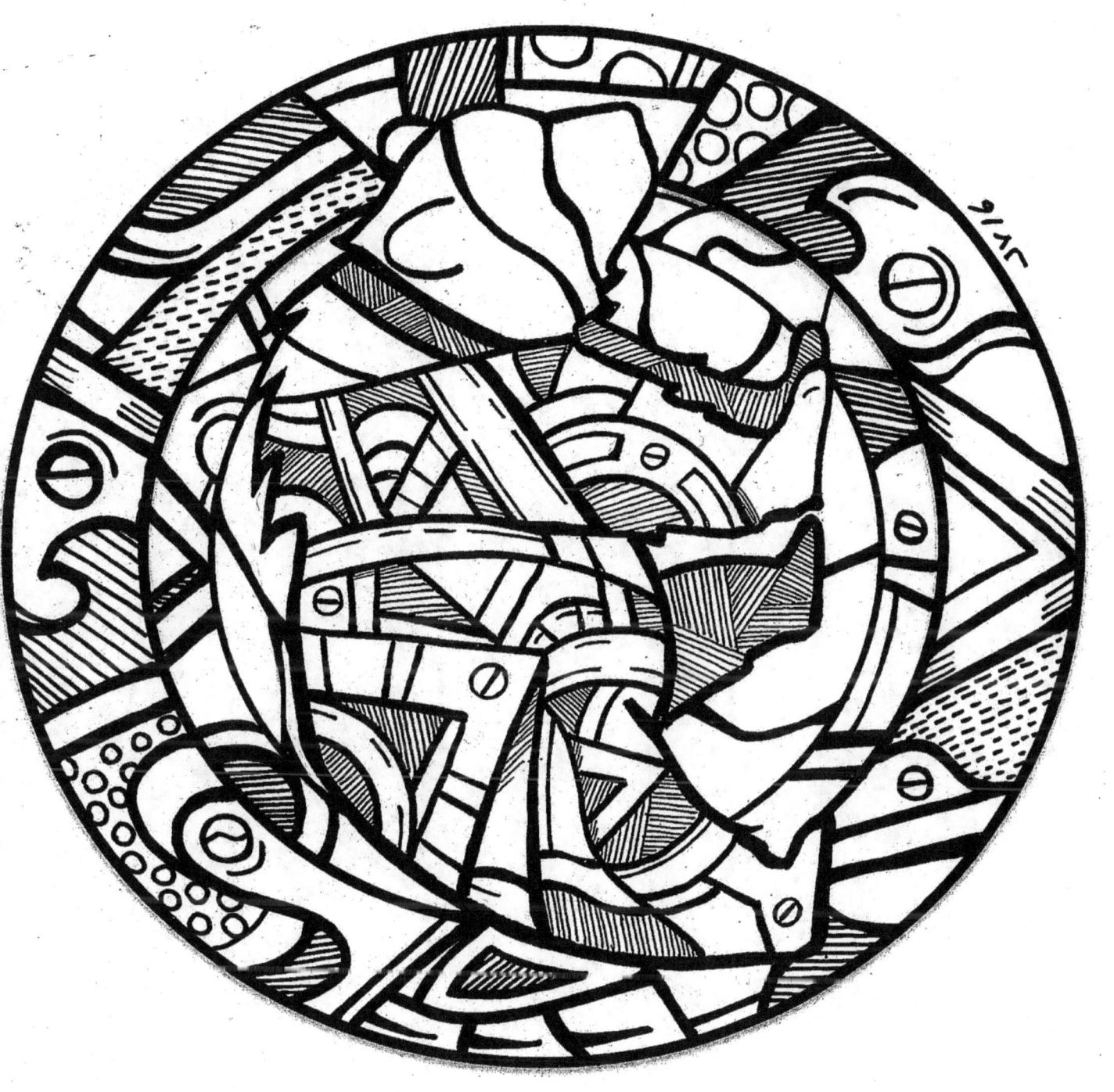

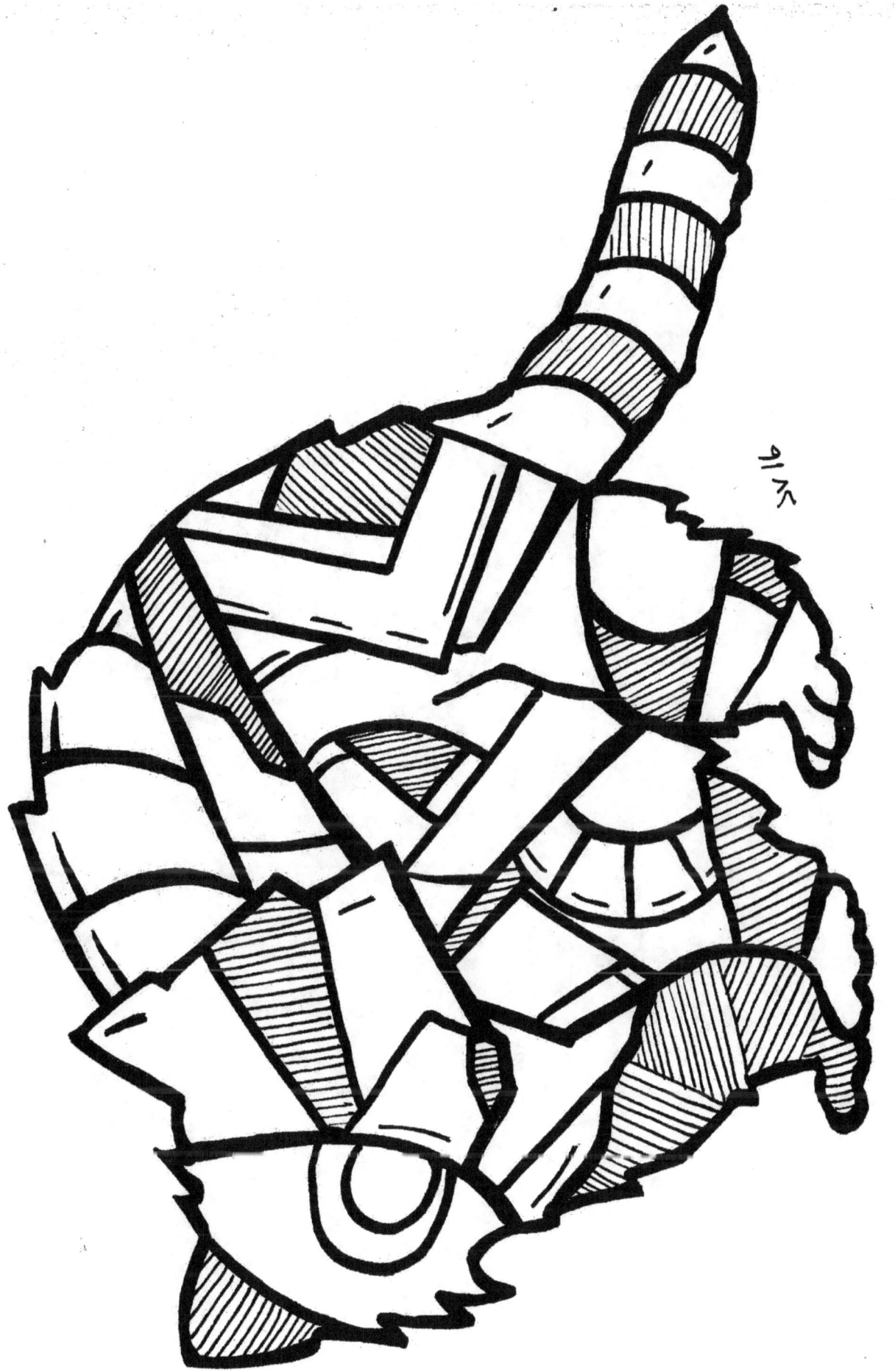

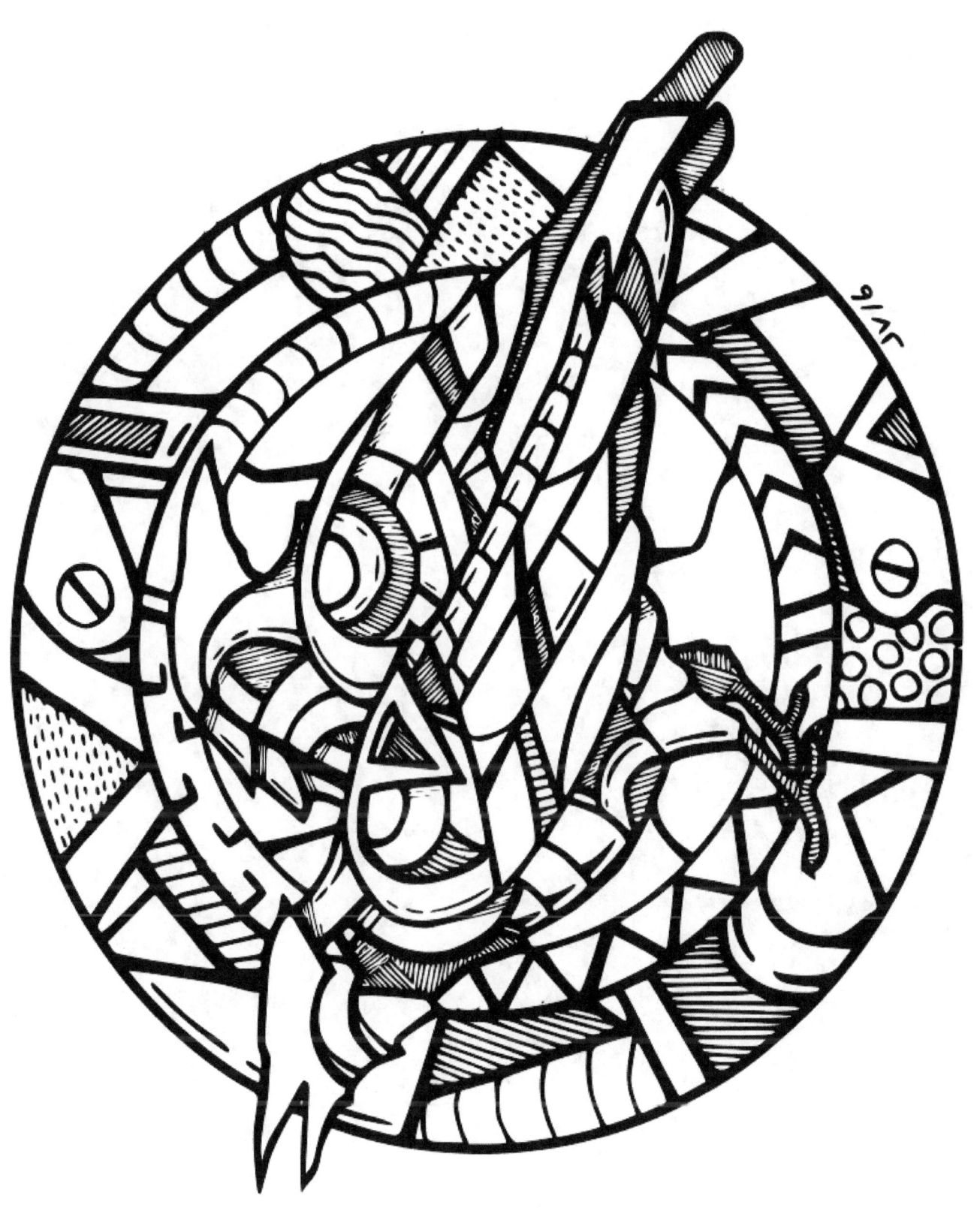

This Book is dedicated to all my family and friends who have always supported and inspired my art and creativity. JV

The images in this book are all original hand drawings by me; I took the images and created them in different forms and lay outs for your enjoyment, tend to like the more handmade look when it comes to drawings and coloring books. This book is an animal lovers dream it features 30 original drawings of

We suggest that the colorist use some sort of backing like cardboard when coloring to prevent bleed through, especially when using markers.

If you have any questions or wish to contact me do so at:

JVillalba1970@hotmail.com

JVCreative@hotmail.com

You can also message me and check out more of my projects and artwork at:

Facebook, look for JVCretive artist.

On Etsy at JVCreative.

Thank you for your support……..and keep coloring. JV
Look for my other books, Old Country Road, and Aztec and Mayan inspired designs.

Please look for my other coloring books on Amazon...

As a bonus I have included a few drawings from my other titles....I hope you enjoy my art as much as I enjoy making it.

Thank you, JV

From my Book *Cat Country*, now on Amazon by JV creative

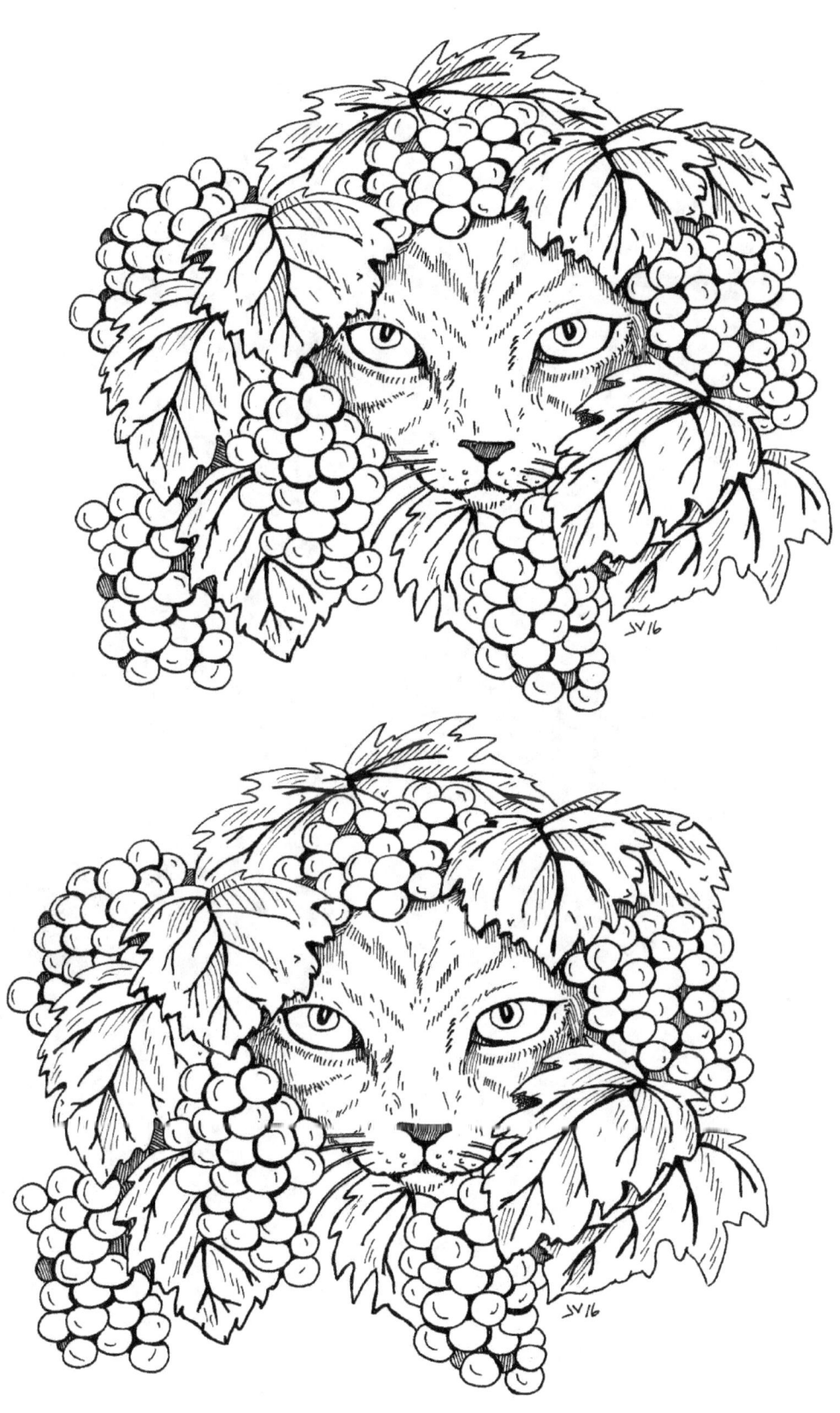

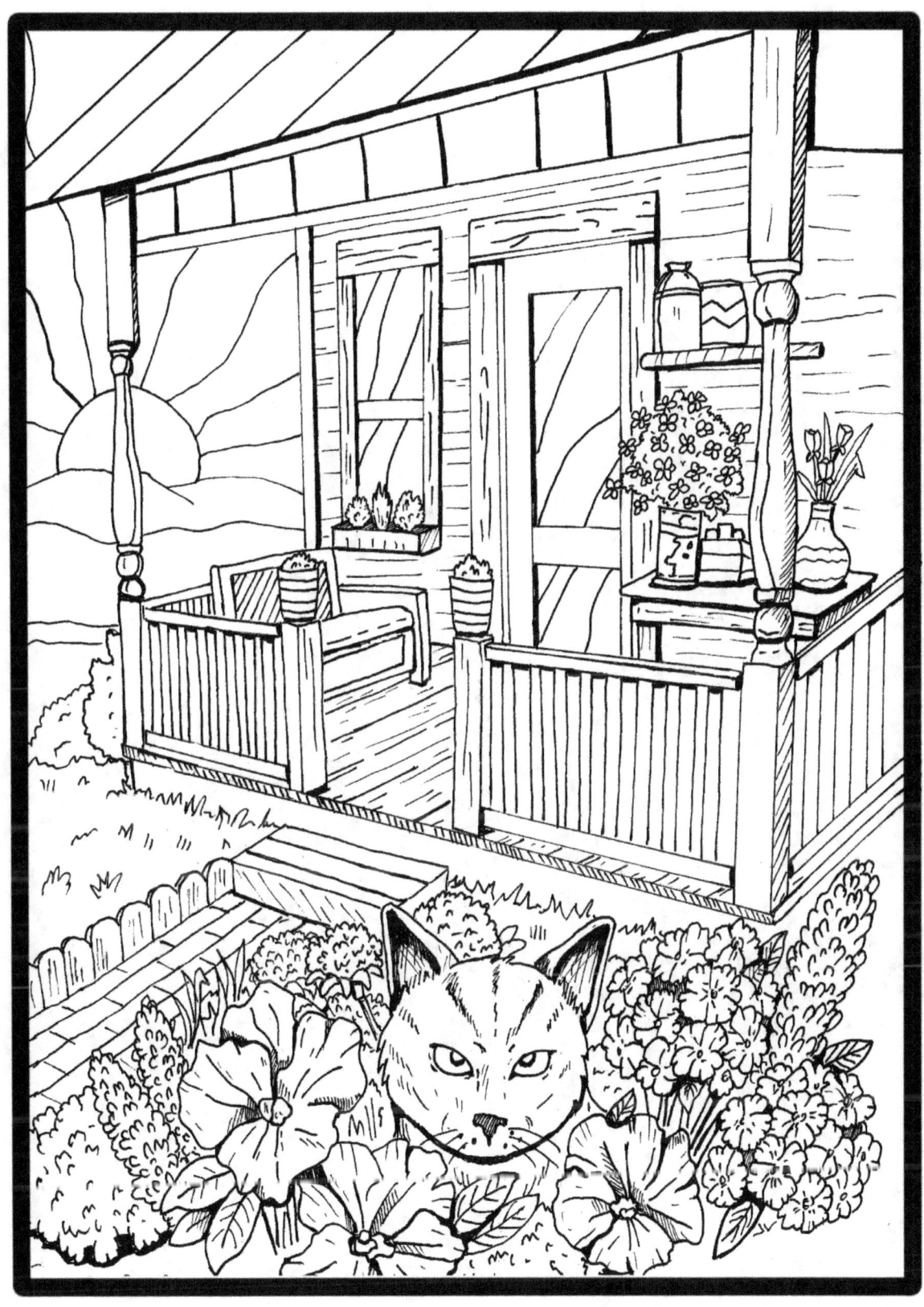

From my Book OLD COUNTRY ROAD Vol.I by JVCreative

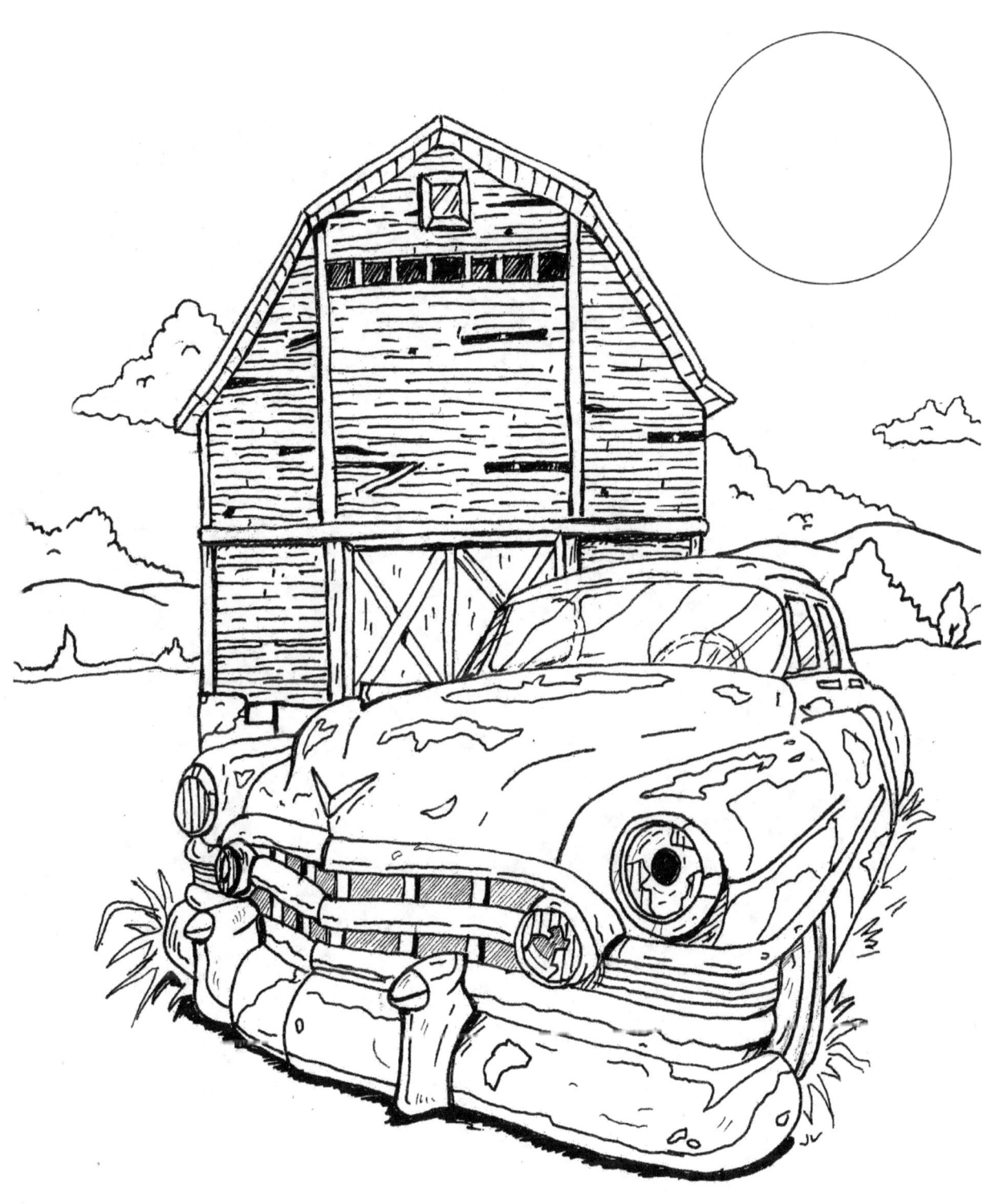

From my book *OLD COUNTRY ROAD Vol. I*, now on Amazon

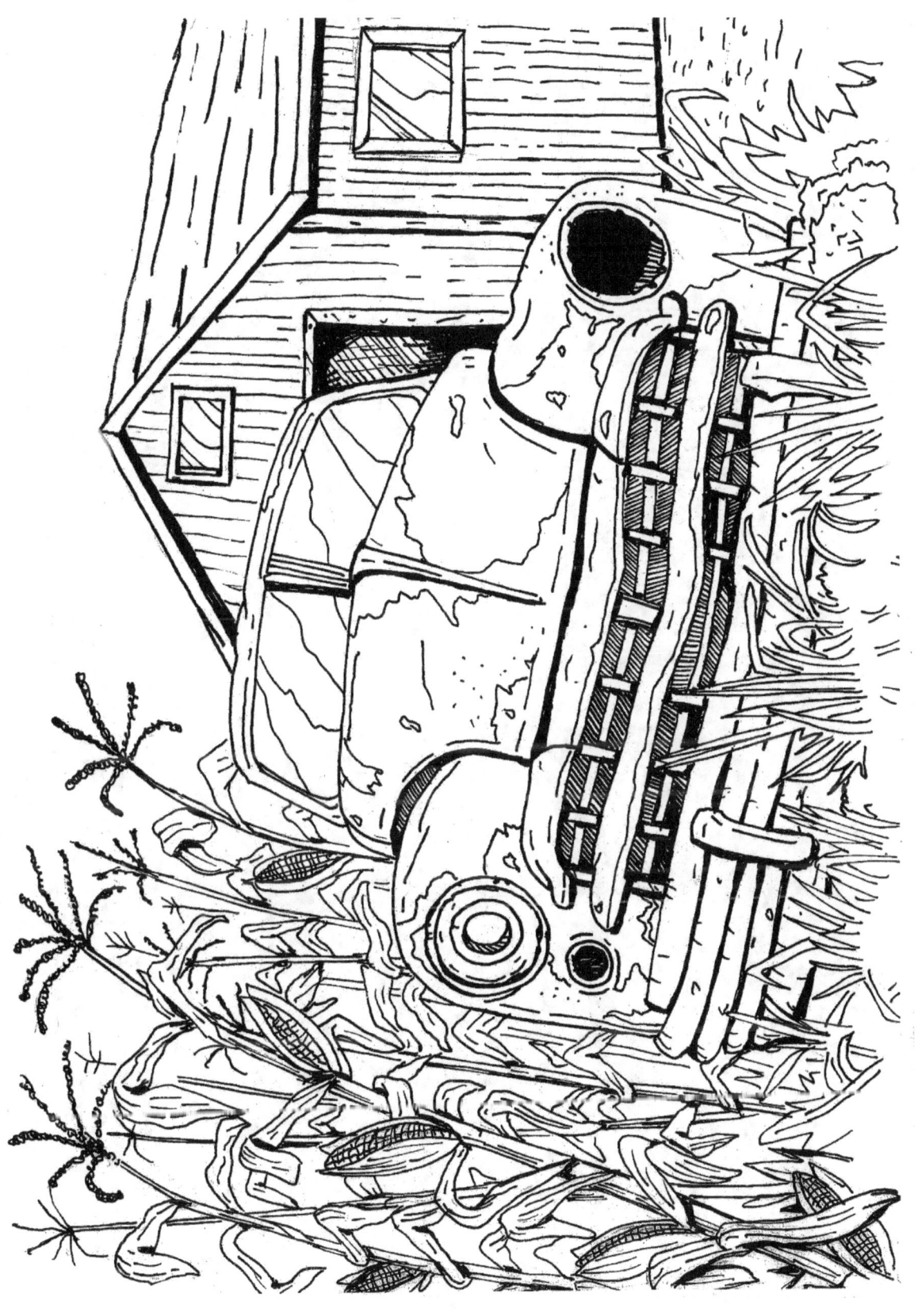

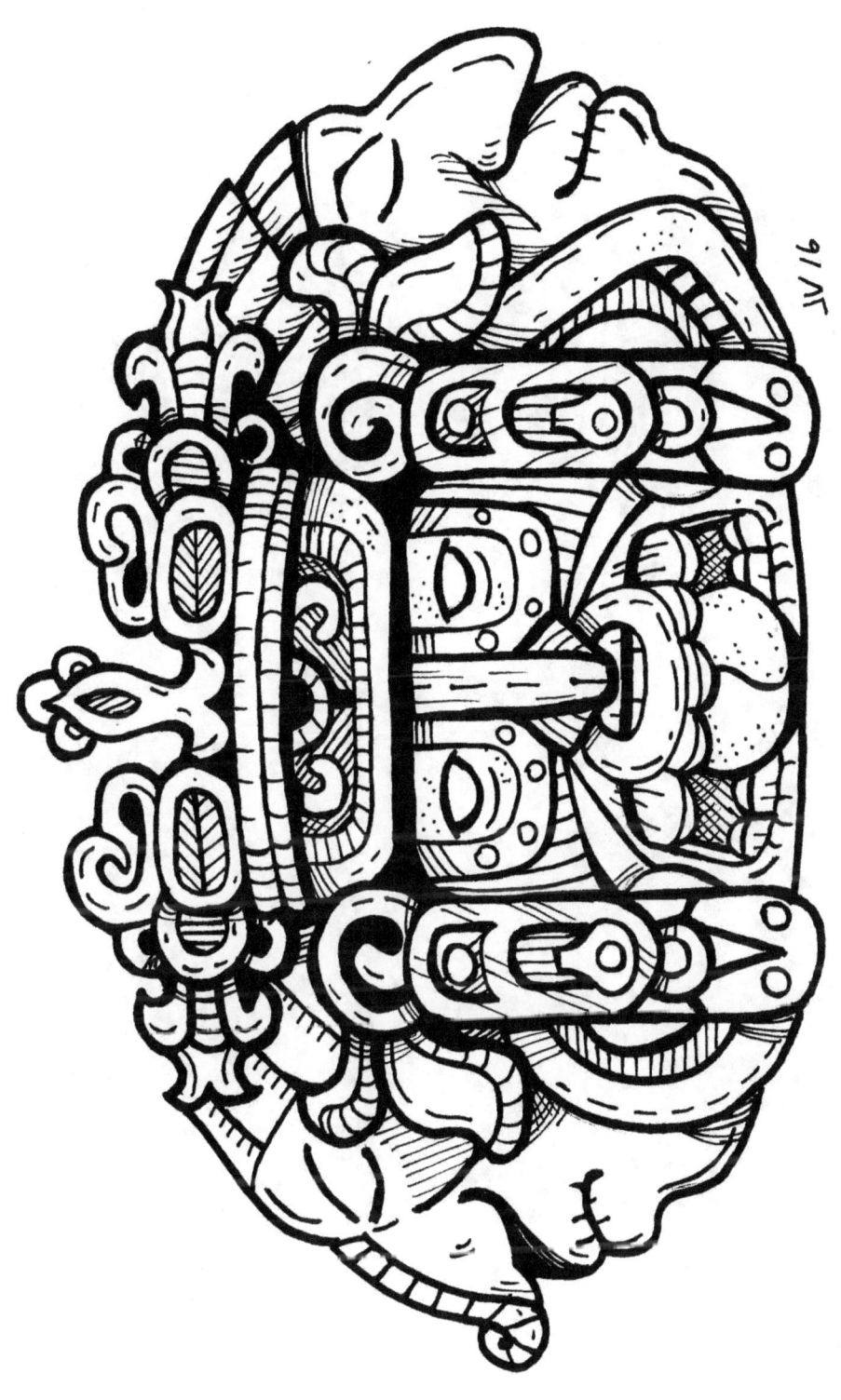

From my book *Aztec and Mayan Inspired Designs.*

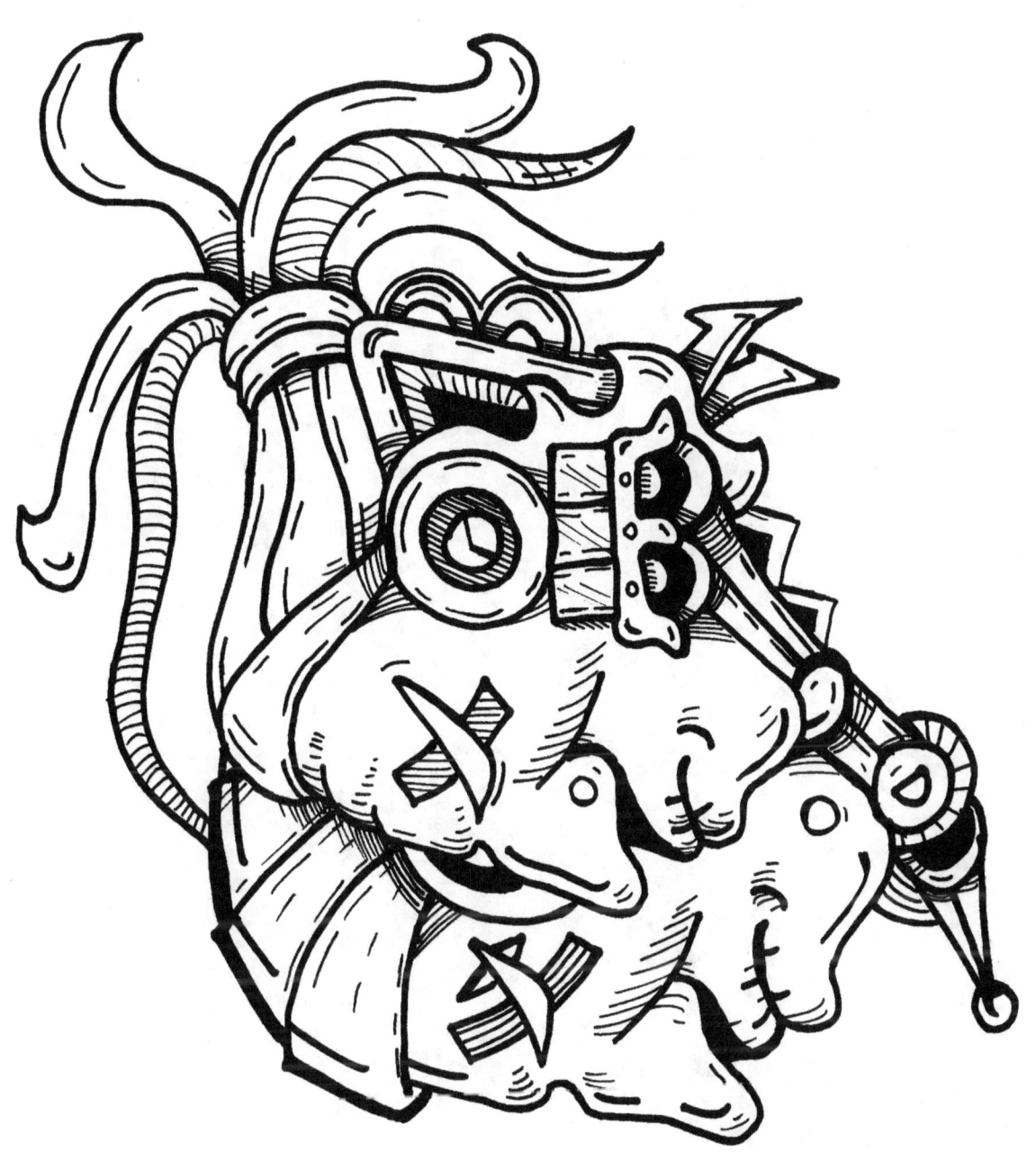

www.ingramcontent.com/pod-product-compliance
Lightning Source LLC
Chambersburg PA
CBHW060012210526
45170CB00017B/2315